KU-827-018

surrounded
by idiots

surrounded by idiots

The Four Types of Human Behaviour
(or, How to Understand Those Who
Cannot Be Understood)

thomas erikson

Vermilion
LONDON

12

Vermilion, an imprint of Ebury Publishing,
20 Vauxhall Bridge Road,
London SW1V 2SA

Vermilion is part of the Penguin Random House group of companies
whose addresses can be found at global.penguinrandomhouse.com

Penguin
Random House
UK

English translation by Martin Pender and Rod Bradbury

Thomas Erikson has asserted his right to be identified as the author of this
Work in accordance with the Copyright, Designs and Patents Act 1988

First published in Sweden as *Omgiven av idioter* by Hoi Förlag in 2014
First published in the United States by St Martin's Essentials in 2019
First published in the United Kingdom by Vermilion in 2019

www.penguin.co.uk

A CIP catalogue record for this book is available from the British Library

ISBN 9781785042188

Printed and bound in Great Britain by Clays Ltd, Elcograf S.p.A.

Penguin Random House is committed to a
sustainable future for our business, our readers
and our planet. This book is made from Forest
Stewardship Council® certified paper.

Contents

Foreword

Many years ago, Bill Bonnstetter and his son David developed a revolu-
tionary software system based on the DISC method—a way of describing
human communication and classifying behavior and the method that is
used throughout this book. Sadly, Bill has since passed away, but David
continues to run their company—TTI Success Insights—to this day. From
its humble origins in rural Iowa, this method of behavior profiling has
now been used by businesses and corporations all around the world.

It all began with one question. A simple, specific question: Could an
agricultural salesperson sell more seed simply by looking at a farm?

As a child growing up in rural Iowa, I watched my father apply
the foundational principles of William Moulton Marston's *Emotions of*
Normal People. At the time, my father was focused on Buyer Profile
Blending, giving agricultural salespeople the knowledge of Marston's
tools to better understand themselves and their farmer customers.
I can still recall the earliest days, sitting at a knotty-pine table over
meals of hot pork tenderloins and roast corn, when my father was
working through his observations. "Pristine driveways and neat

groves? Definitely a Blue. New and experimental livestock and buildings? You're looking at a Red."

Although we were close, our paths were incredibly different. My father, a true entrepreneur and Red/Yellow in every sense of the phrase, was driven to build consulting firms and agencies that helped salespeople refine their craft. I sought the collegiate path, attending university at the University of Iowa, leaning into my Red/Blue nature while studying accounting and computer science. I spent my free time in the computer lab, pouring my soul into programs through my fingertips. While I was studying, my father perfected his wizardlike ability to understand people.

My father and I always remained close and spoke to each other most weeks, even though we were at different milestones in our lives. While I was studying at the University of Iowa, my father sat me down and asked me about contributing to his venture. He asked, "What if we could couple your ability to develop software with my ability to analyze human behavior?" I was ambitious, hungry for fun coding work, and proceeded to embark on the most exciting journey of my life. Together, we built a software system that would produce reports about human behavior. This was a multiplying factor; soon we were able to reach more people and reveal a person's potential through 3.5-inch floppy disks and twenty-four-page reports. My father and I built a company, TTI Success Insights, in 1984 in Iowa to do just that.

Over time, we escaped the frigid winters in the Midwest of the United States, relocated ourselves, our families, and our business to sunny and warm Scottsdale, Arizona. In the late nineties, we began using the web for distribution of our famed assessments. Today, we have a thriving business with distributors all over the world.

Up until now, you might have wondered why you are so different. Human behavior is, for the most part, complex and nebulous. In some cases, the people around us are idiotic. Understanding human behavior is a never-ending task, an endless pursuit to know the how, what, and why behind a person's choices. It is both easy and dangerous to categorize someone who behaves differently from you as ignorant, wrong, or even thickheaded. Today's world requires a more sophisticated understanding where you value a person for his or her strengths and weaknesses.

My father has since passed on. But the purpose we invoked, to reveal human potential, continues to live on. This book is written about the concepts my father applied in sales trainings and applies them to an even more complex situation—understanding the idiots who surround us all.

As you read, I think you will understand the worth of a Red, a Yellow, a Green, and a Blue. I hope you will pull away some practical advice in communicating effectively with each type. But the most important lesson that you can walk away with is that the idiots who surround you are, in fact, not idiots at all. Instead, they are individuals worthy of respect, understanding, and being valued.

Anyone can use the frameworks outlined in this book to get ahead in the game of life. And look at it this way: If you don't understand and use the principles, you'll continue to be surrounded by idiots. And nobody wants that.

—David Bonnstetter
Chief Executive Officer
TTI Success Insights

Introduction

The Man Who Was Surrounded by Idiots

I was in high school when I first noticed that I got along better with certain people rather than others. It was easy to talk to some of my friends; in any conversation, we always found the right words and everything just flowed smoothly. There were never any conflicts, and we liked one another. With other people, however, everything just went wrong. What I said fell on deaf ears, and I couldn't understand why.

Why was speaking to some people so easy, while others were total blockheads? Since I was young, this certainly wasn't something that kept me awake at night. However, I still remember puzzling over why some conversations flowed naturally, while others didn't even start—no matter how I conducted myself. It was just incomprehensible. I began using different methods to test people. I tried to say the same things in similar contexts just to see what reaction I got. Sometimes it actually worked and an interesting discussion developed. On other occasions, nothing happened at all. People just stared at me as if I were from another planet, and sometimes it really felt that way.

When we're young, we tend to think of things very simply. Because some people in my circle of friends reacted in a normal way that meant, of course, that they were automatically the good guys. And so I just assumed there was something wrong with the people who didn't understand me. What other explanation could there possibly be? I was the same all the time! Certain people just had something wrong with them. So I simply began to avoid these weird, difficult people because I didn't understand them. Call it the naïveté of youth if you will, but it did give rise to some amusing consequences. In later years, however, all of this changed.

Life went on with work, family, and career, and I continued to pigeonhole people into two groups—good and sensible people and all the rest, the people who didn't seem to understand anything at all.

When I was twenty-five years old, I met with a man who was self-employed. Now in his sixties, Sture had founded his own business and built it up for many years. I was given the task of interviewing him just before a new project was to be implemented. We started talking about how things were functioning in his organization. One of the very first comments Sture made was that he was surrounded by idiots. I remember laughing at the time because I thought it was a joke. But he truly meant what he said. His face turned crimson as he explained to me that the people working in Department A were complete idiots, every single one of them. In Department B you found only fools who understood nothing at all. And he hadn't even come to Department C yet! They were the worst of all! They were so weird that Sture couldn't fathom how they even made it to work in the mornings.

The more I listened to him, the more I realized that there was something very odd about this story. I asked him if he really believed that he was surrounded by idiots. He glared at me and explained that very few of his employees were worth having.

Sture had no issue letting his employees know how he felt. He didn't hesitate in the least to call anyone an idiot in front of the whole company. This meant that his employees learned to avoid him. No one dared to have one-to-one meetings with him; he never got to hear bad news because he would often shoot the messenger. At one of the offices, a warning light had even been mounted at the entrance to the building. Discreetly placed above the reception desk, the light went red when he was there and turned green when he was away.

Everyone knew about this. Not only staff but even clients would automatically cast a nervous glance at the light to find out what awaited them when they stepped over the threshold. If the light was red, some people would simply turn back at the door, deciding to come back at a more opportune time.

As we all know, when you're young you are full of great ideas. So I asked the only question I could think of: "Who hired all these idiots?" I knew, of course, that he had hired most of them. What was worse was that Sture understood exactly what I had implied. What I implicitly asked was: Who is actually the idiot here?

Sture threw me out. Later on, I was told that what he really wanted to do was fetch a shotgun and shoot me.

This incident got me thinking. Here was a man who would soon retire. He was obviously a proficient entrepreneur, highly respected for his sound knowledge of his particular line of business. But he couldn't handle people. He didn't understand the most critical, complicated resource in an organization—the employees. And anyone he couldn't understand was simply an idiot.

Since I was from outside the company, I could easily see how wrong his thinking was. Sture didn't grasp that he always compared people to himself. His definition of idiocy was simply anyone who didn't think or act like him. He used expressions that I also used to use about certain types of people: "arrogant windbags," "red-tape jackasses," "rude bastards," and "tedious blockheads." Although I never called people idiots, at least not so they could hear me, I had obvious problems with certain types of people.

It was an utterly appalling thought to have to go through life

INTRODUCTION

constantly thinking that I was surrounded by people who were impossible to work with. It would make my own potential in life so unbelievably limited.

I tried to see myself in the mirror. The decision was easy to make. I didn't want to be like Sture. After a particularly toxic meeting with him and some of his unfortunate colleagues, I sat in the car with a lump in my stomach. The meeting had been a total disaster. Everyone was furious. There and then I decided to learn what is probably the most important knowledge of all—how people function. I would be encountering people for the rest of my life, no matter what my profession was, and it was easy to see that I would benefit by being able to understand them.

I immediately began to study how to understand the people who initially seem so difficult. Why are some people silent, why do others never stop talking, why do some people always tell the truth while others never do? Why do some of my colleagues always arrive on time, while others rarely manage to? And even why did I like some people more than others? The insights I gained were fascinating, and I've never been the same since I began this journey. The knowledge I acquired has changed me as a person, as a friend, as a colleague, as a son, as a husband, and as the father of my children.

This book is about what is perhaps the world's most widely used method to describe the differences in human communication. This method is called the DISA—an acronym that stands for Dominance, Inducement, Submission, and Analytic ability—system. These four terms are the primary behavior types, which describe how people sees themselves in relationship to their environment. Each of these behavior types is associated with a color—Red, Yellow, Green, and Blue. This system is also commonly called the DISC system, where the final letter of the acronym stands for Compliance instead of Analytic ability. I have used variations of this tool for over twenty years with excellent results.

But how do you become really, truly proficient at handling different types of people? There are, of course, various methods. The most common method is to research the matter and learn the basics. But learning the theoretical part doesn't make you a world-class communicator. It's only when you begin using this knowledge that you can develop real and functioning competence in the field. Just like learning to ride a bike—you have get on the bike first. Only then do you realize what you need to do.

Since I began studying how people function and painstakingly strove to understand the differences in the way we communicate, I've never been the same. I'm not as categorical anymore, judging people just because they are not like me. For many years now, my patience with people who are the complete opposite of me has been far greater. I wouldn't go so far as to say that I never get involved in conflicts, just as I wouldn't try to convince you that I never lie, but both these things happen very seldom now.

I have one thing to thank Sture for—he awakened my interest in the subject. Without him, this book would probably never have been written.

What can you do to increase your knowledge about how people relate and communicate? A good start may be to keep reading this book—the whole book, not just the first three chapters. With a little luck, in a few minutes you can begin the same journey I began twenty years ago. I promise you will not regret it.

One thing to note: To simplify reading this book, I have chosen to use "him" and "he" consistently when I refer to examples not associated with any specific person. I know that you have enough imagination to insert a "her" or "she" in your thoughts where this may be appropriate.

Surrounded
by Idiots

1

Communication Happens on the Listener's Terms

Does that sound strange? Let me explain. Everything you say to a person is filtered through his frames of reference, biases, and preconceived ideas. What remains is ultimately the message that he understands. For many different reasons, he can interpret what you want to convey in a totally different way than you intended. What is actually understood will, naturally, vary depending on who you are speaking to, but it is very rare that the entire message gets through exactly as you conceived it in your mind.

It may feel depressing knowing that you have so little control over what your listener understands. No matter how much sense you would like to knock into the other person's head, there's not that much you can do about it. This is one of the many challenges of communication. You simply can't change how the listener functions. However, most people are aware of and sensitive to how they want to be treated. By adjusting yourself to how other people want to be treated, you become more effective in your communication.

Why Is This So Important?

You help other people understand you by creating a secure arena for communication—on their terms. Then the listener can use his energy to understand rather than to consciously or unconsciously react to your manner of communicating.

All of us need to develop our flexibility and so be able to vary our style of communication, adapting it when we speak to people who are different from us. Here we find another truth: No matter what method you choose to communicate with, as an individual, you will always be in the minority. No matter what kind of behavior you have, the majority of people around you will function differently from you. You can't just base your method of communication on your own preferences. Flexibility and the ability to interpret other people's needs is what characterizes a good communicator.

Knowing and understanding another person's style of behavior and method of communication will result in more educated guesses about how a person may possibly react in various situations. This understanding will also dramatically increase your ability to get through to the person in question.

No System Is Perfect

Let me be clear about one important point: This book doesn't claim to be totally comprehensive with respect to how we, as people, communicate with each other. No book can do that, because the number of signals we constantly transmit to those around us wouldn't fit into any book. Even if we could include body language, the differences between male and female dialogue, cultural differences, and all the other ways to define variations in communication, we wouldn't be able to write everything down. We could add psychological aspects, graphology, age, and astrology and still not get a 100 percent complete picture.

According to the *American Journal of Business Education* (July/August 2013), more than 50 million assessments have been made using the DISA tool. And yet even with all this information communication remains a fascinating and puzzling topic. People are not Excel spreadsheets. We can't calculate everything. We're way too intricate to be described in full. Even the youngest child is far more intricate than anything that could be conveyed in a book. However, we can avoid the most blatant blunders by understanding the basics of human communication.

It's Been Going On for a While

"We see what we do, but we do not see why we do what we do. Thus, we assess and appraise each other through what we see that we do."

These words come from the psychoanalyst Carl Jung. Different behavior patterns are what creates dynamism in our lives. When I refer to behavior patterns, I don't just mean how a person acts in a single instance (his actions) but rather the whole set of attitudes, beliefs, and approaches that govern how a person acts. We can recognize ourselves in certain behavior patterns, but other forms of behavior we neither recognize nor understand. Besides, each of us acts differently in different situations, which can be a source of either joy or irritation for those around us.

Though individual actions can, of course, be right or wrong, there is really no pattern of behavior that is right or wrong. There is no such thing as proper behavior or incorrect behavior. You are who you are, and there's no point in wondering why. You're fine no matter how you're wired. No matter how you choose to behave, no matter how you are perceived, you are fine. Within reasonable limits, of course.

In a perfect world, it would be easy just to say, "I'm a particular kind of person and it's okay because I read it in a book. That's just how I am and this is how I act." Sure, wouldn't it be great not to have to mishandle your own behavior? To always be able to act and behave precisely as you feel at the time? You can do that. You can behave exactly as you wish. All you have to do is find the right situation in which to do so.

There are two situations in which you can just be you:

The first situation is when you're alone in a room. Then it doesn't matter how you speak or what you do. It doesn't hurt anyone if you scream and swear or if you just want to sit silently and ponder the great mysteries of life or wonder why fashion models always look so mad. In your solitude, you can behave exactly the way you feel. Simple, isn't it?

The second situation where you can completely be yourself is when all the other people in the room are exactly like you. What did our mothers teach us? Treat others as you want to be treated. Excellent advice and very well intentioned. And it works, too—as long as everyone is just like you. All you need to do is make a list of all the people you know who believe, think, and act exactly like you in all situations. Now just give them a call and start hanging out.

In any other situation, it might be a good idea to understand how you are perceived and to learn how other people function. I don't think I will make headlines by saying that most people you meet aren't like you.

Words can have incredible power, but the words we choose and how we use them vary. As you have seen from the title of this book, there are different interpretations of—yes, you got it—words. And when you use the wrong word, well, maybe then you're an idiot.

Surrounded by Idiots–or Not?

What does this actually mean? As I was writing, the following analogy hit me: Behavior patterns are like a toolbox. All types are needed. Depending on the occasion, a tool can sometimes be right and sometimes be wrong. A thirty-pound sledgehammer is great for tearing down walls, but it's hardly the thing if you want to hang a picture in the foyer.

Some people are opposed to the idea of sorting people into different behavior types. Maybe you believe that you shouldn't categorize people in that way, that it's wrong to pigeonhole people. However, everyone does it, perhaps in another way than I do in this book, but we all register our differences nonetheless. The fact remains that we are different, and in my opinion, pointing that out can be something positive if you do it in the right way. Improperly used, every tool can be harmful. It's more about the person using it than the tool itself. This book is your introduction to human behavior and dialogue. The rest is up to you.

Parts of what you are going to read I have gathered from TTI Success Insights. I would like to take this opportunity to thank Sune Gellberg and Edouard Levit for so generously sharing both their experience and their training materials.

No Matter How Strange It Might Seem, in Theory, Every Kind of Behavior Is Normal

Normal Behavior...

. . . is relatively predictable.

Every person reacts in a habitual manner in similar situations. But it's impossible to predict every possible reaction before it happens.

. . . is part of a pattern.

We often react in consistent patterns. Therefore, we should respect one another's patterns. And understand our own.

. . . is changeable.

We should learn to listen, act, speak openly, and reflect in order to do what is relevant right now. Everyone can adapt.

. . . can be observed.

We should be able to observe and consider most forms of behavior without being amateur psychologists. Everyone can take note of the people around them.

. . . is understandable.

We should be able to understand why people feel and do what they do—right now. Everyone can think about why.

. . . is unique.

Despite the conditions that we have in common, each person's behavior is unique to him. Succeed in your own conditions.

. . . is excusable.

Dismiss personal jealousy and complaints. Learn to have tolerance and patience, both with yourself and with others.

2

Why Are We the Way We Are?

Where does our behavior come from? Why are people so different? Search me! Very briefly, it's a combination of heredity and environment. Even before we're born, the foundations for the behavior patterns we will exhibit in adulthood have been laid. The temperament and character traits we have inherited affect our behavior, a process already begun at the genetic stage. Exactly how this works is still a bone of contention among scientists, but all are in agreement that it does come into play. Not only do we inherit traits from our own parents but also from their parents—also in varying degrees from other relatives. At some point or other, we have all heard that we speak like or look like an uncle or an aunt. As a child, I resembled my uncle Bertil—something to do with my red hair. To explain how this is genetically possible would take a tremendous amount of time. For the moment, let us just establish that this inheritance lays the foundation for our behavioral development.

What happens once we are born? In most cases, children are born impulsive, adventurous, without any barriers whatsoever. A child does exactly what he wants. The child says, "No, I don't want to!" or,

"Sure I can!" He is immersed in the thought that he can manage just about anything at all. This kind of spontaneous and sometimes uncontrolled behavior is, of course, not always what his parents wished for. Then, hey presto, what was once an original pattern of behavior begins to transform, in the best/worst-case scenario, into a copy of someone else.

How Are Children Influenced?

Children learn and develop in multiple ways, but the most common is by imitation. A child mimics what he sees around him, the parent of the same sex often becoming the model for imitation. (This is clearly not an exhaustive study on how the process works, as this book is not about how we influence our children.)

Core Values

My core values are found deep within me, values so deeply embedded in my character that it's almost impossible to change them. These are the things I learned from my parents as a child or that I learned in school when I was very young. In my case it was different variations of "study and do well in school" or "fighting is wrong." The latter, for example, means that I've never laid hands on another person. I haven't fought since third grade, and I seem to recall that I lost then. (She was really strong.)

Another important core value is that all people are of equal worth. Because my parents demonstrated this to me during my childhood, I know it is deeply wrong to judge a person based on his or her origin, sex, or color. All of us carry many such core values. We know instinctively what is right and what is not. No one can take these core values away from me.

Attitudes and Approaches

The next layer is my attitudes, which are not exactly the same thing as core values. Attitudes are things I have formed opinions about based on my own experiences or on conclusions I have drawn from encounters in the latter part of my schooling, high school, college, or my first job. Even experiences later on in life can form attitudes.

A relative once told me that she didn't trust salespeople. She's definitely not alone in having strong feelings about salespeople, but in her case it resulted in comical practices. She couldn't buy anything without returning it. A sweater, a sofa, a car—the buying process was endless. Every fact had to be examined and explored. No matter how much research she did beforehand, she always wanted to return her purchases afterwards.

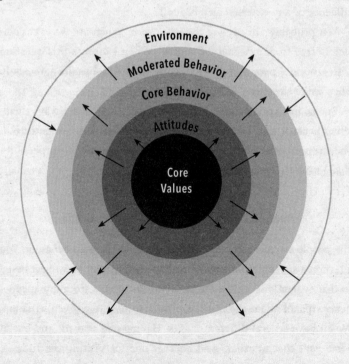

Once I had observed the pattern, I asked her why she did this, and she explained the reasoning behind her attitude: Eighty-five percent of all salespeople were swindlers. Explaining that I too was a salesperson had little effect. To this day, I don't know if I belong to the 85 percent or if I can count myself among the fortunate 15 percent. The important thing is that an attitude can change. My relative had probably been badly fooled a number of times and therefore learned to distrust salespeople. However, if she had a number of positive experiences her opinion could change.

The Results

Both my core values and my attitudes affect how I choose my behavior. Together they form my core behavior, the real person I want to be. My core behavior is how I act in complete freedom, without the influence of any external factors at all.

You probably already see the issue here: When are we ever completely free from external influences? When I discuss this question with groups of people in different contexts, we all usually agree: only when we're sleeping.

But people are different. Some don't care. They are always themselves because they've never reflected upon how they are perceived. The stronger your self-understanding is, the greater your probability of adapting to the people around you.

How Do Others Really Perceive Me?

The people around you most often see your moderated behavior. You interpret a specific situation and make a choice about how to act based on that evaluation—this is the behavior that others around you experience. It's all about the mask you wear to fit into a given situation. We all have several different masks. Having one at work and one at home isn't that unusual. And another one for visiting the in-laws, perhaps. This book is not an advanced course in psychology—but I am content to establish that we interpret situations differently and act accordingly.

Consciously or subconsciously, surrounding factors cause me to choose a particular course of action.

And this is how we act. Look at this formula:

BEHAVIOR $= f(P \times Sf)$

Behavior is a function of *Personality* and *Surrounding factors*.
Behavior is that which we can observe.
Personality is what we try to figure out.
Surrounding factors are things that we have an influence on.

Conclusion: We continually affect one another in some form or other. The trick is to try to figure out what's there, under the surface. And this book is all about behavior.

3

An Introduction to the System

At the end of this book you will find a description of the background to how the DISA system emerged, but since you probably want to dive into its most interesting elements—how everything works in practice— you can just read on. Otherwise, you can always go directly to page 228.

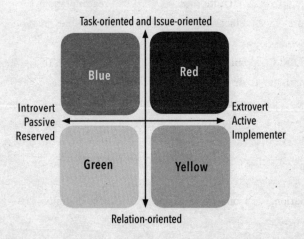

ANALYTICAL (blue)
- Slow reaction
- Maximum effort to organize
- Minimal interest in relationships
- Historical time frame
- Cautious action
- Tendency to avoid involvement

DOMINANT (red)
- Quick reaction
- Maximum effort to control
- Minimal interest for caution in relationships
- Current time frame
- Direct action
- Tendency to avoid involvement

STABLE (green)
- Calm reaction
- Maximum effort for connection
- Minimal interest in change
- Current time frame
- Supportive action
- Tendency to reject conflict

INSPIRING (yellow)
- Rapid reaction
- Maximum effort to involve
- Minimal interest in routine
- Future time frame
- Impulsive action
- Tendency to reject isolation

As you can see, there are four main categories of behavior types, each of which is associated with a color. This book is about how you can recognize them. Quite soon, as you start reading about the different colors, various faces will come to mind. Sometimes, maybe, even your own.

About 80 percent of all people have a combination of two colors that dominate their behavior. Approximately 5 percent have only one color that dominates behavior. The others are dominated by three colors. Throughout the book I focus on the single colors individually because they are the fundamental components of a person's behavior. It's like a recipe—we need to understand all the ingredients before we bake the cake. Entirely Green behavior, or Green in combination with one other color, is the most common. The least

RED	YELLOW	GREEN	BLUE
Aggressive	Talkative	Patient	Conscientious
Ambitious	Enthusiastic	Relaxed	Systematic
Strong-willed	Persuasive	Self-controlled	Distant
Goal-oriented	Creative	Reliable	Correct
Pushing	Optimistic	Composed	Conventional
Problem-solver	Social	Loyal	Seems insecure
Pioneer	Spontaneous	Modest	Objective
Decisive	Expressive	Understanding	Structured
Innovator	Charming	Lengthy	Analytical
Impatient	Full of vitality	Stable	Perfectionist
Controlling	Self-centered	Prudent	Needs time
Convincing	Sensitive	Discreet	Reflecting
Performance-oriented	Adaptable	Supportive	Methodical
Powerful	Inspiring	Good listener	Seeks facts
Results-oriented	Needs attention	Helpful	Quality-oriented
Initiator	Encouraging	Producer	Scrutinizes
Speed	Communicative	Persistent	Follows rules
Timekeeper	Flexible	Reluctant	Logical
Intense	Open	Thoughtful	Questioning
Opinionated	Sociable	Conceals feelings	Meticulous
Straightforward	Imaginative	Considerate	Reflecting
Independent	Easygoing	Kind	Reserved

common is entirely Red behavior, or Red behavior in combination with one other color.

Many people you meet possess qualities that you sometimes wish you had—you may even feel jealous of these people. They easily master things that you struggle with. Maybe you'd like to be more decisive like Reds, or maybe you wish it were easier for you to interact with strangers, like Yellows. Possibly, you wish that you didn't stress so much, that you could just take it easy like Greens do, and perhaps you wish that you could keep your schedule in better order, something that's natural for Blues.

Naturally, it works the other way as well. You are going to read things that will help you realize that you too boss others around a bit too much, just like Reds tend to do. Or that you talk way too much, something that Yellows do. It might be that you take things way too easy, not getting involved in anything, the Greens' weakness. Or you're always suspicious of everything, seeing risks everywhere, just like Blues. Here you can learn to see your own pitfalls and how you can take appropriate measures to get around them.

No matter what you learn about yourself and others, take notes, underline things, and engage with the material.

4

Red Behavior

How to Recognize a Real Alpha and Avoid Getting in His Way

What should we do? We'll do it my way. Now!

This is the behavior type that Hippocrates in his theory of human temperament called choleric. Nowadays you might call a Red person bold, ambitious, driven, but also potentially hot-tempered, rash, or dominant. You quickly notice a Red person because he doesn't make the slightest effort to conceal who he is.

A Red person is a dynamic and driven individual. He has goals in life that others may find difficult to even imagine. Since his goals are so highly ambitious, achieving them seems to be impossible. Reds strive forward, always pushing themselves harder, and they almost never give up. Their belief in their own ability is unsurpassed. They carry inside them the firm belief that they can achieve anything—if they just work hard enough.

People who have lots of Red in their behavior are task-oriented extroverts and they enjoy challenges. They make quick decisions and are often comfortable taking the lead and taking risks. A common perception is that Reds are natural leaders. These are people who willingly take command and go to the fore. They are so driven that they will get through despite any obstacle in their path. Their disposition is ideal in competitive situations. It's not unusual for a CEO or a president to have lots of Red in his behavior.

This form of competition is present in everything Reds do. To say that they constantly want to challenge and compete is probably not entirely true, but if a chance of winning something arises—why not? The exact nature of the competition is unimportant; it's the competitive element that keeps Reds running on all cylinders.

Pelle, one of my former neighbors, liked competing so much that he developed entirely new interests just to compete. I like working in the garden, and so I spend quite some time doing so. Pelle didn't like gardening, but when he had heard people commenting on my beautiful garden often enough he finally had enough. He started one project after another, always with a single but very clear objective: to outdo me. He confounded his wife by digging new flower beds, planting a rainbow of unbelievably fabulous plants, and cultivating the lawn to golf-course standard. The only thing I needed to do to keep him going was to merely suggest that I would purchase more plants. Then he would go to the local garden center quicker than you could say "bad loser."

You can also recognize Reds by other behavior patterns. Who talks the loudest? Reds. Who goes all out when explaining something? Reds. Who's always the first to answer a question? Reds again. Who, during an otherwise pleasant dinner, makes categorical comments on just about any topic? And who will judge an entire country based on something he saw on television? Reds!

Something is always happening in the lives of Red people. They can't sit still. Idle time is wasted time. Life is short; better get going immediately. Do you recognize the type? Always on the go. So step aside; let's get cracking!

"Tell Me What You Really Think—Yes, for Real."

Reds have no problem being blunt. When asked a specific question, they often say exactly what they think, without any frills. They see no need to wrap things up in a bunch of empty phrases. When a thought pops into their heads, everyone knows it immediately. They have opinions on most things, and they trot their thoughts out quickly and efficiently.

A common remark is that Reds are very honest, because they dare to express their personal truths to people. They don't really understand what the fuss is all about. They've only said things as they are.

If you need someone with extra energy, you may want to invite a Red into the team or project group. They fight tirelessly along when others have already given up—if they are determined to succeed, that is. A task that has become humdrum or meaningless could be totally ignored by a Red.

I call this phenomenon slog or split. If the task is important enough, a Red will go through fire and water to complete it. If he feels it has no purpose, into the trash it goes.

RED people often see themselves as:

Driven	Resolute	Ambitious
Decisive	Competitive	Independent
Prompt	Determined	Time-conscious
Persuasive	Strong-willed	Results-oriented

Can I Win Something? In That Case, I'm In.

So Reds like competing. They appreciate the slight antagonism that is part of being competitive and the glorious moment of winning. They even enjoy winning competitions that probably don't even exist, except perhaps in their own mind. It can be passing a slow walker on the street, finding the absolutely best parking spot, or dominating the family game of Monopoly—despite the fact that the purpose of the game is to entertain the kids and none of the other adults are actually competing. For a Red, this is all natural because he sees himself as a winner.

Let me give you an example. I once worked for a company where the CEO was Red. He was energetic and efficient—and consequently incredibly dynamic. No meetings were as short and sweet as those run by this CEO. But his weak spot was the competitive element. As a young man he had played soccer, and every spring at this particular workplace they held a soccer tournament. It was very popular, even before he joined the company.

Naturally, he had to take part. No other CEO before him had ever done so, but that wasn't the problem. The problem was that as soon as he got out on the field he became a different person. On fire with his competitive drive, he flattened anyone who stood in his way.

This continued for a few years until someone had the guts to tell him that he played just a little bit too rough—the game wasn't supposed to be that serious. The CEO didn't understand. He grabbed the latest flyer for the game and pointed out that it was called a soccer "tournament." Tournaments are competitions, and if you compete you are in it to win. Simple!

He competed in traffic, on the soccer field, in business. No area was too insignificant not to become a competition. He even raced to see how quickly he could finish reading a book. What others do for relaxation he transformed into a competition. One hundred pages an hour was a reasonable pace.

His wife had even banned him from playing a memory card game with his children, who were five and six years old. Since they had better memories than he did, they won most of the time, and in his frustration he intimidated them.

Before you conclude that this guy sounds rather unsympathetic, we need to look at his intentions. This kind of intensive and competitive behavior often upsets other people because they think it is all about dominating and suppressing others. Nothing could be further from the truth. His intentions were almost never malicious. He just wanted to win.

This is one of the greatest challenges for Reds. It's not uncommon that other people feel irritated or intimidated by them because they're such powerful personalities. Later on in this book, I will share some simple ways that you can deal with these individuals.

Time Is Money

"Quick" is synonymous with "good" for Reds. If you are in a meeting and suddenly notice that one of the other participants is devoting his time to something completely different, it may well be a Red who has lost interest. If you look closer, you will realize that his thoughts are elsewhere—on the next step in the process being discussed, for example. Because Reds are quick thinkers, they move on long before everyone else.

Few things annoy Reds more than sluggishness. If a meeting or a discussion drags on, he may interrupt and ask if it's really necessary to prolong the issue. "We've already discussed this for twenty minutes. Get it together! It's only a few million in investments. How hard can it be?"

If you think about it, they're often right. When other people may find it difficult to make a decision, Reds are prepared to make quick decisions in order to keep things moving. With a Red on the team, nothing will be discussed ad infinitum. After all, it's always better to do something rather than nothing, right?

The advantage is obvious. We're talking about people who never waste time on anything that doesn't move forward. As soon as a task becomes unclear or is taking too long, a Red will ensure that the momentum is maintained and spur things along. Chop-chop, done in double time.

About fifteen years ago I began working for a small consulting company with about a dozen employees. It was a polished organization with a great spirit of entrepreneurship and excellent momentum in business dealings. One of the reasons why they were so efficient was because the founder of the company was a Red. Nothing could move too quickly for Björn. No meeting took longer than was absolutely necessary.

In my second or third week in the new job, I was sitting in a traffic jam when my cell phone rang. I looked at the display and saw that it was Björn. I answered the way I'd been instructed to when I started at the company—with a greeting, my name, and the company name. Impatiently he interrupted me and spit out his question.

"Were you looking for me?"

"No," I replied, and took a deep breath, ready to say something else. I didn't get the chance.

"Okay," he said, and hung up.

Eight seconds.

Unpleasant? Well, at the time we didn't really know each other. However, I must admit that the whole episode had me worried a little—at least on that occasion. Only three weeks at the company and the big chief himself calls, and sounding irritated!

When we'd gotten to know each other—and I learned that Björn was Red—I asked him why he was so abrupt on the phone. Of course he didn't even remember the call, but he said he was probably just trying to find out if I was looking for him. When he learned I wasn't, there was no further need to talk. Wasting time on polite flowery phrases or drawn-out farewells wasn't for him.

But at the same time, here was a person with a capacity to work far more than normal. Björn managed to do more in an average working day than most people. He still has an exceptional ability to make the most of any free time. If he has a gap of five minutes in his schedule he manages to squeeze in an email, a phone call, and go through some meeting minutes. From the outside, this may seem like an unnecessary pursuit of efficiency. But a Red detests inactivity. Things must happen. Add to this a sense of constant urgency, and a great deal will get done.

The Sky's the Limit. Or Is It?

For a Red, a realistic budget is a budget for cowards. If we don't push ourselves to the breaking point, we haven't tried hard enough. Reds love difficult tasks, so their level of ambition is usually boundless. The ability to manage difficult situations and challenges is the defining attribute of Red behavior.

When a person with Red traits sets his goals, several things happen. First, he wants to know how well a specific task under the most favorable conditions could be performed. If all nineteen parameters were met and we all gave it a little extra effort the results would be phenomenal. This means that anything below that impossible level of excellence is boring, because there's at least a remote possibility of that result being achieved.

Nothing is impossible. The impossible just takes a little longer. More than likely it was a Red who came up with that expression.

Naturally, it's also about the type of project. It's not enough just to set an impossible sales budget. If a Red doesn't like sales, he'll ignore the budget. Since he prefers to make all the decisions himself, he probably won't be fooled into doing something he doesn't feel like doing.

Reds set higher demands on themselves than any of the other colors would. And they are always prepared to work hard. I wouldn't go so far as to say that no other color works as hard as Reds do, but I would venture to say that a Red would give anyone a run for his money.

Ambition, which is intrinsic to Reds, shouldn't be confused with a lust for power. Reds have no problem taking positions of power, since they are fearless. Expressions like "It's lonely and windy at the top" don't scare them. But for a Red power is not an end in itself. It does, however, come in handy for those who like to make their own decisions and avoid having to wait for others.

A Red can, in fact, be quite unassuming. It's true that he has a strong ego, but status and prestige don't have the same importance as with other colors. The reason is simple: A Red usually doesn't care what others think. He's not here for their sake—he's here for his own.

Let Me Tell You How Things Really Are

A Red gives everything he's got. When he has an opinion about something or if he wants the rest of us to agree with him, he pulls out all the stops.

Once, I was in a meeting with a large number of people who didn't know one another that well. It was a gathering of consultants who were meeting to discuss a potential collaboration. It was in the middle of a recession, and we were all concerned about the lack of direction. While we were waiting for the chairperson to arrive, we chatted a little about everything.

At one end of the table sat Elisabeth, who had strong opinions about everything. In an unequivocal voice, she suddenly stated that the company was still expected to earn over $50 million a week, despite the recession. About fifteen consultants, all highly trained, reflective, and intelligent people, nodded in agreement. Just imagine—$50 million! Per week!

While Elisabeth expanded on how the situation ought to be resolved in the consulting world, I began thinking about the figures a little bit. Not knowing where these figures came from, I remained silent. It could be true; it could also be farfetched. I honestly didn't know. While waiting for the meeting to begin officially, I started calculating how much $50 million per week would be per year. I didn't have enough paper.

After the meeting, I got the answer to my speculations. I was in a taxi on my way to my next meeting when the driver turned on the radio. In the news, it was announced that the company in question was expected to earn between $2 and 2.5 million per week. I realized that Elisabeth had gotten the information from the news. I also understood that $2 or $2.5 million per week was far more realistic than the $50 million that she had referred to.

But wait a minute. A little reconciliation with reality is needed here. Why didn't anyone react? No one in the room lifted a finger or called her information into question. Why?

Because she sounded so convincing! Her facial expression was definite; her countenance was determined, and her voice did not quiver in the least when she presented her figures.

That's the way Reds function. When they believe something, they let people know that this is the only truth that exists. Now maybe there are some sticklers for detail who might claim that this is deceptive, since we now know that the company earned $2.5 million a week and not roughly $50 million. But I'm convinced that Elisabeth really believed what she said. She had things turned around, no doubt about that, and she was certainly not interested in details. But my point is that by sounding utterly confident when she declared that the company was earning six months' revenue—per week—we all fell for it.

Or, in the words of a good friend of mine: There are two ways to do this—my way and the wrong way.

Only Dead Fish Go with the Flow

Reds are both groundbreaking and strong willed. Why not also add "results oriented" and "decisive" when we're at it? For Reds, it's not sufficient to do things like everyone else does. And just because it's tough doesn't mean we should avoid doing it.

Reds aren't afraid to make decisions. When everyone else hesitates, thinking and weighing the risks, a Red makes the controversial decision. A Red's determination is usually unyielding. Once he's decided, then it's full steam ahead.

Their fearlessness dares them to tackle things that make others hesitate. This is usually evident when things get rough, and they are undaunted by tough choices or tricky decisions. It is no coincidence that many entrepreneurs are Reds. Setting up new businesses—especially if they are based on completely new business concepts—is, in our current economy, not for the faint of heart. It's not a bad thing to have a force of nature in the driver's seat. It takes a strong mind to move things forward, someone who understands that risks that are part of everyday life and that everything boils down to hard work from morning to night—for many years. Reds understand this from the beginning and are in no way intimidated by it.

Do you need someone to pursue a problem in your apartment complex? Maybe you've gotten on the wrong side of your landlord, who says that there is absolutely nothing wrong with your heat. Or maybe the contractor who repaired the roof and installed the new elevators was negligent and won't take responsibility for it. Any time you try to get things straightened out, you've been brought to standstill by a barricade of unanswered calls and info@ addresses. You're just about to give up when you suddenly remember the guy on the second floor living above you. Isn't he kind of Red? Wasn't he the one who dared to go against the super at the last meeting and get the trash policy changed? Yes, that's the guy!

Throw the guy from the second floor into the process, and then you'll see things begin to happen. You might have to motivate him a little, explaining that he has a lot to gain from it himself. But he will make things happen—he'll subdue the landlord and get the contractor in line. And he won't lose any sleep just because someone got angry with him in the process.

Generally speaking, a Red's strengths are very powerful. They are extremely clear in their communication, and you don't have to look far to identify Red behavior. Of course, over the years many Reds learn to restrain themselves somewhat, but it doesn't usually last very long. They'll be back to full throttle—and all that that entails.

It Wasn't Better Before. Onward and Upward.

A Red doesn't try to stick to his original point of view when he realizes that a better solution exists. He is a quick thinker and has no problem shifting his ground at short notice. One of the advantages of this is that he doesn't reject other people's ideas if he has none himself. It's worth looking into anything that can propel development forward.

Sometimes decisions can come a little bit too quickly, but the will to constantly change creates a strong dynamism and flexibility. If anything has been static for a long time—maybe a few weeks—he will turn things up a notch. Some people may find this stressful, but when you ask a Red why he changed something that was actually working the answer could well be "Because I could."

Naturally, there are also downsides. Reds get bored with the status quo quickly and so they change it—the people around them have no idea what will happen next. When Greens and Blues have just gotten used to the new organization and think they have finally grasped how things are supposed to work, well, a Red will have already outlined the next step.

Conclusions on Red Behavior

So what do you think? Do you know any Reds? Do you have any around you? If you want to get to know some famous Red people, consider Steve Jobs, FDR, Venus Williams, or Margaret Thatcher. There's also Barack Obama and Mother Teresa.

Oh yes, it's true. If you consider Mother Teresa's deeds, the strength she needed and whom she had to deal with—the world's foremost leaders—to achieve what she did, then you'll realize that she was extremely determined and forceful. A typical Red profile.

5

Yellow Behavior

How to Recognize Someone Whose Head Is in the Clouds and Get Him Back to Reality Again

"That Sounds Fun! Let Me Do It!"

In the Hippocratic world, we have now come to the sanguine person. What other words can be used to describe him? Optimistic and cheerful, a person with a bright outlook on life. The thesaurus even suggests the epithet a man of possibilities . . . how about that? It is, in fact, an excellent description of Yellow behavior. These are people who live to live, always finding opportunities for enjoyment. Life is a banquet, and Yellows will see to it that they savor every bite. They are driven by merriment and laughter. And why not? The sun is always shining somewhere.

Do you know anyone who sees sunshine where others see dark clouds? Have you met anyone who can laugh even though he hasn't had any good news for months? Then you've met a Yellow. Have you been at a party and wondered why everyone flocks around a particular person, man or woman? Well, in the center of the circle there's a Yellow, entertaining anyone who wants to laugh. Yellows make sure that the atmosphere is at its zenith so that every event becomes a marvelous party. When something is no longer fun, they move on to another place where the atmosphere is better.

Recognizing a Yellow is easy. He's the one who's talking all the time. He's the one who gives answers rather than asking questions—often answering questions that no one has even asked. He answers a question by telling a story that may or may not have anything to do with the issue. But it really doesn't matter, because he will put you in a cheerful mood. Besides, his unshakably positive attitude also makes it impossible for you to feel upset for long.

I would even go so far as to argue that Yellows are more popular than other colors. How can I say that? Look for yourself. They entertain, put people in a good mood, and fun things always happen around them. They know how to capture everyone's attention and how to keep it. They make us feel important. They are just nice to be around.

They are also very typically touchy-feely people. Like Reds, Yellows are very willing to make quick decisions, but they can rarely explain why using rational reasoning. A more likely response would be, "It just felt right." And sure, gut feelings shouldn't be underestimated. Studies have shown that gut feelings are right more often than we think. But that's not the kind of gut feeling we're talking about here. Yellows often make decisions that are based on feeling simply because no thought was ever involved.

I have a sister who is Yellow. Marita is so easygoing in her manner that I have never heard anyone utter a single negative word about her. Never. I may be biased, but I have never met anyone who doesn't immediately like her. She has an entirely unique ability to connect with every person she meets.

Marita always has something entertaining to say. However, some of these things are so peculiar that I sometimes have to ask her what she was thinking when she said them. With a burst of laughter, she usually replies, "Thinking? I wasn't!"

In many ways, it's liberating when I visit her and her husband, Leif.

Their almost incomprehensible ability to see bright spots in everything around them is so delightful that it frees my own easygoing disposition. I am never as happy and exhilarated as when I visit them. For years, I wondered why this was, and have reached the conclusion that Yellow behavior is simply contagious.

If I say to my sister, "It looks like it is going to rain," she simply replies, "I can't imagine that." Pointing to the window, I say to her, "But look, it's actually raining. It is quite dark out there; we could have thunder before this is over." "Sure," she says, "but after that the sun will come out! Just wait and see." Then she laughs. Again. While the rain pours outside, she sits on the sofa, unabashedly having fun. And I, along with everyone else, laugh along because it's impossible to resist.

"The More the Merrier! Your Friends Are My Friends. . ."

People with lots of Yellow in their behavior are focused on creating relationships. They are outgoing and can be extremely persuasive. They're enthusiastic, excited, and happy to talk about their feelings for others and, not infrequently, for complete strangers.

Yellows can talk to anyone. They are not at all shy, perceiving most people they meet as pleasant. They even see strangers in a positive light—they're just friends you haven't met yet.

Many people notice that Yellows are always smiling and laughing. That's undoubtedly one of a Yellow's strengths. Their optimism is invincible. Comments about how everything is going to hell are often met by remarks about "What a beautiful view we have!"

Just like Reds, Yellows have lots of energy. They find most things interesting, and Yellow individuals are the most curious people you'll ever meet. Everything new is enjoyable, and a great deal of Yellow energy is spent finding new ways of doing things

Who gets the most holiday cards, do you think? Yellows. Most contacts in their cell phone? That's right—Yellows. Most friends on Facebook? You're getting the idea—Yellows. They have friends absolutely everywhere, and they are excellent at keeping in touch with everyone in order to keep up-to-date. Yellows want to know what's going on. They want to be where it's all happening, and they will make sure to be at every party.

YELLOW people often see themselves as:

Enthusiastic	Charming	Outgoing
Inspiring	Optimistic	Flexible
Open	Creative	Spontaneous
Convincing	Easygoing	Communicative

"Isn't It Amazing? I Loooove It to Bits!"

If there is anything that characterizes Yellow behavior, it's unlimited optimism and enthusiasm. Few things can keep their good mood away for long. The Yellows' entire being is concentrated on one thing—finding opportunities and solutions.

In his day, Hippocrates called Yellows the sanguine ones. This simply means optimists. Nothing is really a problem. It will all sort itself out. It's neither here nor there that the world just happens to be full of worries and hardships. With their incurably positive outlook on life, Yellow individuals give joy to the people around them with their cheerful acclamations and entertaining jokes.

I don't know where Yellows get their tremendous energy, but it's focused on having fun and devoting themselves to social togetherness. Everyone must be involved, and a Yellow will not allow anyone to be gloomy.

Micke, a good friend of mine, is Yellow, and his life has included more than his fair share of challenges. His wife left him, his children have had problems at school, and on various occasions his employers have gone bankrupt and he has lost his job. I can't even count how many times he's had a car accident, his home has been burgled, or he has been robbed of expensive items. Sometimes I hardly dare to answer the phone when I see that Micke is calling. To tell the truth, Micke is the most jinxed man I have ever met.

But what's so curious about him is that none of this ever seems to bother him. Naturally, he's upset when accidents happen, but he can't stay upset for long periods of time. Inside, he just bubbles along most of the time.

I remember one occasion when we were both quite young. He had just bought an old Alfa Romeo. It was a two-seater with two doors. Painfully rusty, it was nothing short of a miracle that it even held together. Micke had the car for about a week when he hit a lamppost and couldn't get out on the driver's side. When I heard about the accident, I was worried and called to see if he was okay. His answer? "It was fine! I just got out the other door!"

The Optimistic Consultant
Strikes Again

Since Yellow individuals are so positive and cheerful, they spread joy and warmth to those around them. With their uncontrollable optimism, they demolish all opposition quite effectively.

Who can be upset when there's someone pointing out the good things all the time?

How could anyone fail to be inspired by a person who refuses to see half-empty glasses? Who always sees the positive?

One of my customers is a sales director for a pharmaceutical company. Marianne worked her way up in the company via what we call the long route. Her managers and coworkers all agree that she's been so successful simply due to one thing: her amazing ability to inspire those around her.

On a number of occasions, I've watched her conduct sales meetings. I consider myself a decent motivator, but when Marianne gets going you just have to take your hat off to her. Within a couple of minutes, the room is so inspired if she were to ask the sellers to jump out the window they'd do it, even though they are on the fifth floor. She makes everything sound so simple.

"It's a great idea to jump out the window! We can do this. Let's jump!"

And the group jumps after her. With her optimism and bright outlook on life, she is phenomenal at getting people to achieve great feats— just by closing their eyes to anything negative. With sheer inspiration, she can inflate people's confidence to incredible levels.

I once saw her dealing with an irate customer who felt mistreated by her organization. Not a situation most people dream about! It turned out it wasn't a problem for Marianne. By just smiling steadfastly at the customer and refusing to listen to his negative comments, she moved him from an angry face to a gentle smile and finally to boisterous laughter. How could that happen? I don't think that even she could explain the underlying process. It simply came naturally to her.

What Happens If We Turn Everything Upside Down?

You won't find anyone more resourceful than a Yellow. If there is anything Yellows have an aptitude for, it's seeing solutions where others do not. Yellows have the unique ability to twist and turn things. To put it simply, they turn everything upside down and think outside the box. Call it what you want, but their thinking doesn't always follow any set pattern.

They move quickly: The Yellow's intellect is very fast, which means that it can be difficult to keep up. Sometimes they can even find it difficult to explain their wild ideas.

A good friend of mine likes to work on his home. Everything relating to interior design and garden design fascinates him. I suspect that Robban would secretly rather work in design on a full-time basis instead of his actual job.

I've seen this for myself, but I've also heard from his wife how he goes about things. He walks around the garden, and she starts counting backwards from ten. On seven, Robban says, "Honey, I have an idea."

There are a few reasons for Robban's creativity. It's easy for him to think in images. He can simply "see" things in front of him long before they even exist. And he has courage; he's not afraid to try new things. Or to talk about them. Usually, his mouth works parallel to his mind as he discovers these ideas.

I've worked with a Yellow who couldn't even cross the street without coming up with a few really thought-provoking business ideas—just by looking around. How does this work? I don't really know. For a long time, we asked him to write down his proposals. You'll learn more about how a Yellow would react to that kind of structure when we start talking about weaknesses.

Yellows are also helped by the fact that they rarely have any limitations. A Yellow dares to go beyond the usual conventions when he's in a creative mode. Normally, of course, structure and hierarchy in a business are a kind of limitation, but Yellows are rarely concerned about such things. In fact, they often don't seem to know that such limitations are there.

Need help with new suggestions or ideas? Hunt out the most Yellow person you know. Are you stuck in the same way of thinking? Do you need a new perspective on an old problem? Speak to a Yellow. You might not be able to use whatever idea scheme they come up with—in fact, realism isn't a factor for a Yellow—but one thing can lead to another and then all of a sudden you have something that works.

Selling Snow to a Penguin

With all their energy and optimism, Yellows are very persuasive. It's easy for them to get carried away, seeing opportunities and solutions where others might only see a dead end.

It's often said that there is a difference between convincing and persuading, and many Yellows cross these boundaries. But what they say sounds so good. With the help of language, they really are masters at winning over people to their side.

Regarding language: As I describe in the chapter on body language (page 106), most Yellows have a rich and varied way of gesticulating, so that they can convince you not just with their words, but with their entire bodies.

But it's not just energy and will. Yellows have a unique way of expressing themselves that sways their listeners. They often use vivid and colorful imagery when they speak, which appeals to all five senses and creates an impression that is felt by the whole body.

Without even knowing it, many Yellows are skilled rhetoricians. They know instinctively that their ethos, the bearer of the message, is just as important as the message itself. Therefore, they are mindful of getting through to you as an individual—usually by being friendly and shaking your hand; making small personal comments; making you feel important.

Many politicians are phenomenal at this—think of Bill Clinton, for instance. He has the kind of charisma that is naturally present in many Yellows—a noticeable interest in another person, the ability to ask exactly the right questions so that others feel that they are important.

"I Know Lots of People. All of Them, in Fact."

If Yellows aren't allowed to cultivate their relationships, they will slowly wither and die. Okay, this may be somewhat exaggerated, but the very definition of Yellow behavior revolves around their ability to build relationships.

The Yellow traits are inspirational. They inspire those around them, and the best way to achieve this is through building relationships. A Yellow knows that by far the most important factor in business, for example, is relationships. If your customer doesn't feel positively about you, it will be difficult to make any headway.

Yellows know everyone. They have more acquaintances than everyone else. They like everyone. A Yellow doesn't need to know a person very well before calling him his friend. Anyone who doesn't actively dislike them they consider to be a pal. Remember that when Reds ask *what* is going to be done, Yellows want to know immediately *who* will do it. This question is crucial for Yellows. If the team or group does not function smoothly, a Yellow will not feel well. He needs functioning relationships for him to come into his own.

Conclusions on Yellow Behavior

What do you think? Have you ever met a real Yellow? Famous people who exhibit clear yellow traits include Oprah Winfrey, Robin Williams, Ellen DeGeneres, and, to take some fictional examples, Pippin from *The Lord of the Rings* and Han Solo from *Star Wars*.

6

Green Behavior

Why Change Is So Difficult and
How to Get Around It

"How Are We Going to Do This?
It's Not Urgent, Right?"

The Green person is the most common. You'll meet him virtually everywhere. What's the easiest way to explain who he is? Well, I would like to describe him as being the average of all the other colors. Please don't interpret that as something negative; keep in mind what this truly implies. While Reds are stressed performance seekers, Yellows are creative bon vivant guys, and Blues are perfectionist Knights of Excel Spreadsheets (see pages 13 and 14), Greens are the most balanced. They counterbalance the other more extreme behavioral traits in an elegant way. Hippocrates called them phlegmatic people. The Aztecs called them earth people. Calm, leisurely, and easygoing are some words that could also describe them.

It's just a matter of stating the facts—not everyone can or should be extreme; otherwise, we would never get anything done. If everyone were a driven leader, there would be no one left to be led. If everyone were an enthusiastic entertainer, there would be no one to amuse.

And if everyone were a detail-oriented perfectionist, there wouldn't be anything to keep in order.

This means that Greens don't stick out in the same way as others do and they often lend serenity to a situation. Where Reds and Yellows start off in top gear, Greens are significantly calmer. And where Blues get caught up in details, Greens try to feel their way to what is right.

If you have a friend who is Green, he'll never forget your birthday. He won't begrudge you your successes, and he won't try to take the spotlight off you by reeling off his own stories. He won't try to outdo you, and he will never pester you with new and drastic demands. Nor will he see you as a competitor if you were ever placed in that situation. He won't take command unless he has been told to do so. And he won't—

Just a minute please, you might be thinking. That's just a lot of things he *doesn't* do. So what *does* he do?

You can't ignore the fact that Greens are more passive than others. They're not as driven as Reds, not as resourceful as Yellows, and not as orderly as Blues. This describes most of the population.

For this very reason, they are easy to deal with. They let you be yourself. They don't demand much, and they never kick up a fuss unnecessarily. Children with Green features are usually described as being little angels. They eat when they're supposed to; they sleep when they're supposed to; they do their homework when they're supposed to.

But it's not just that. Greens will not offend people if they can avoid it. They'd rather not offend anyone at all, and they won't talk back if the boss makes a strange decision. (At least not to his face, that is. During the coffee break it may be somewhat different, but more on that later.) They usually strive to fit in, which makes them more balanced people. They're ideal for calming down confused Yellows, for example. And they're excellent at warming up Blues, who, on occasion, can indeed be a tad too cold.

We often hang out with a family where the husband is Yellow and loves to horse around and take center stage—he comes up with amusing games and is more than happy to answer any questions himself. Everyone else is his audience, and he never steps out of the spotlight. His wife is Green. Calm, composed, and as laid back as can be. When he jumps around and frolics (these are middle-aged people), she sits quietly on the sofa and smiles. She's just as entertained as everyone else by his antics. When I ask her if she ever gets tired of her comical husband, she sometimes replies quietly, "But he's having so much fun."

This is a typical Green trait. They are very tolerant towards other people's more singular behavior. Is the picture becoming clearer? Greens are the people you might not think about—most of us, that is.

Some Simple Basics

Green people are kindness personified. You can expect a helping hand whenever you need it. They are pronounced relational people who will do everything within their power to save your relationship. And they will invest lifelong. They will keep track of when your birthday is, when your partner's birthday is, when your children's birthdays are, et cetera. It wouldn't surprise me if they even know when your cat first saw the light of day.

It's often said that Greens are the best listeners, and this is true. A Green will always be more interested in you than in himself, and if perchance he should be interested in himself he would never dream of showing it. You often find Greens in the public sector, where they help others, with no concern for personal gain.

They are also pronounced team players. The team, the group, the family, always comes before the individual, and I would even say that societies consisting of Greens will always take care of the sick and the weak. They will not leave a friend in need; you can call them at any time. They always offer a shoulder to cry on.

Change isn't their greatest strength, even though change isn't completely foreign to them. If you can simply justify the change and give him enough time, even a Green will be prepared to try new things. But a Green will remind you that you always know what you have, but you never know what you might end up with. The grass is not automatically greener on the other side, so to speak.

GREEN people often see themselves as:

Friendly	Calm	Reliable
Considerate	Pleasant	Patient
Predictable	Stable	Team player
Discreet	Thoughtful	Good listener

The Best Pal in the World

As I've already said, these are naturally friendly people. When they tell you that they sincerely care about how you're doing, you can trust that they lie awake sleepless for your sake. Just like Yellows, Greens are relationship people and their interest in others is genuine and authentic.

If you ask a group of people if anyone is prepared to lend a hand and no one steps up to help, a Green will jump in and shout, "Choose me!" Why? Because he didn't want to leave you in the lurch. He knows that if you don't get any help you'll feel bad, and even though he can be passive, he's always prepared to help a friend.

I still remember a young woman I worked with at a consulting firm years ago. Admittedly, Maja was certainly Blue as well, but above all, she was Green. Her problem was obvious: When someone asked for help, she always said yes. Every time.

It was difficult to find her desk due to her workload, but she organized everything in the end. We could always rely on her assistance, handling all the things the rest of us had simply forgotten about. She had a warm and friendly smile, so we asked her to work in reception and have the first contact with new clients. She never failed to serve coffee, fix the cushions, or keep track of how long clients had been waiting.

Maja never forgot anyone's birthday or anniversary (or their wives' or children's, for that matter). She frequently sent short emails to all of us stressed-out consultants reminding us that we had families who also needed to be looked after. Sure, we could take care of our own lives, but in her kindness and thoughtfulness Maja went out of her way to help. It was natural for her, and whenever we asked her to take it easy and take care of herself for a change she almost felt offended. She wanted to take care of us—it simply made her feel good. Of course, there were limits, and Maja constantly ran the risk of someone taking advantage of her huge heart. But when properly balanced, this self-lessness is a beautiful quality.

Greens do this naturally. When having coffee, it's quite normal for you to ask the people with you if they would like a refill. When other colors would likely take their empty cups to the coffeemaker, Greens would simply fetch the coffee carafe and refill everyone's cup.

A Green wants to stay on good terms with everyone, so he'll even help people he doesn't really like that much. Otherwise, there might be some kind of hullabaloo.

He thinks well of most people and is confident in others' abilities. Sometimes he does this so intensely that it ends badly, but normally that's the fault of the other person, not the Green himself. He is so good-hearted that now and then others can take advantage of him.

Lasse, a good friend of mine, is a truly genuine friend. It makes no difference how much he has to do; if anyone needs a helping hand, Lasse is there, ready to support him. Sometimes, in Lasse's eagerness to help with other people's work, he even forgets to do his own.

On weekends, he drives his own and others' children everywhere they want to go. He helps people move; he lends out his tools without people even needing to ask. He listens if you call and complain about something. This all takes a huge amount of time, but he enjoys it.

Once They've Said They'll Do Something, You Can Rest Assured That It Will Be Done

If a Green says that he will do something, you can be confident that he'll do it. If it's in his power to deliver, he will. It won't be done in the shortest amount of time possible, but it will show up in your in-box roughly within the expected time frame. Greens don't want to be caught failing to deliver, as this might cause trouble for others. And because they're good team players, they don't want to do anything that can cause problems for the team. Team comes before self, the team being the company, crew, football team, or family. For the Green, it's natural to look after everyone else around them.

The reason why everyone works so well with Greens is a topic for debate. In some situations, it's simply because they don't like conflict. Mostly, however, it's because they're controlled by their desire to make those around them happy and satisfied. If they can please you with a job well done, they'll do it. The desire to please others verges on being a driving force for Greens. It comes naturally and requires no effort. And this selflessness is accompanied by an exalted serenity that lowers the stress level of those around them.

"We Don't Want Any Unpleasant Surprises. It's Good to Know What's Going to Happen. Every Time."

You can always count on a Green person. In some organizations, it's a requirement to have reliable employees. Creativity and ingenuity are not at the top of the wish list: In short, you simply need people who understand the job and get it done without a lot of fuss or drama.

Then you hire Greens. They constitute the stable core who will do the job well. They don't have problems taking orders—as long as the orders are formulated in an appealing fashion. Greens enjoy stability and a certain predictability in the workplace. Or in the home. Or with the family. Just about everywhere.

Whenever trouble is brewing—maybe due to a recession or when new managers take over—we'll see all kinds of interesting behavior in a group. Reds, who never listen to the whole message, just rush off to do what they believe needs to be done. Unless, of course, they're busy yelling at the management because they don't agree with their decisions. Yellows start wild discussions and inform absolutely everyone about their take on what happened. Instead of working, they'll debate the news until it's time to leave the office. Blues will sit at their desks and begin the bureaucratic paperwork, formulating half a million questions that no one knows the answers to yet.

Greens? They just murmur. If the management has avoided seriously sabotaging their sense of security, they'll trundle on without complaining. There's no point in making a lot of fuss and bother about it. Might as well keep doing what you were before. This, in fact, makes things much easier. We'll get to how we help Greens to change direction, but they're great at keeping calm and carrying on.

You'll always know how a Green will respond to some questions because he doesn't change his opinion very often.

A few years ago, I coached Greger. He had been a CEO for several years, and his management team consisted solely of Green middle managers. He used to enjoy playing a little game when launching new ideas. He wrote little notes with the answers he thought he would get from each person. "No" from Anna. "Yes" from Stefan. "Maybe" from Bertil. Right every time! Greger knew them very well and knew how they would react to his proposals.

This wouldn't have been the case with Yellows. They don't even know how they're going to respond when opportunities arise. Exciting—sure, but it's exhausting for those around them. With Green associates, however, you don't need to worry.

"Who? Me? I'm Not Important. Forget That You Even Saw Me."

For every Green, the group will always come first. Team before self. Remember that. This is a fundamental truth for a Green, and it shouldn't be challenged too strongly. The working group, the team, the club, and the family—all these different groups are important for a Green. He often disregards his own needs if the group gets what it needs.

You may think that groups consist of people and if each individual is satisfied the group as a whole will be content. This might happen, but then the focus would be individual rather than collective. The way a Green sees it, if the group feels good every individual also feels good.

Here the Green's thoughtfulness becomes apparent—he has infinite regard for those around him. This is partly the reason why it's difficult to get a straight answer from a Green. He's always trying to satisfy everyone else.

Let me tell you a rather striking story. One Sunday a few years ago, a colleague whom I didn't know that well called me. I had only been working with Kristoffer for a few months, but I hadn't really figured the guy out yet.

So when he called me one Sunday morning I was surprised. I saw who it was, but I had no idea what he wanted from me. He greeted me pleasantly and asked what I was doing. I had just bought a new house at that time and was busy renovating. Kristoffer asked what was on the agenda this particular Sunday, and I remember that I said I was worried about the boiler. It was early winter. The temperature was just below freezing, and one of the circulation pumps didn't really work as it should. Because colder weather was definitely on the way, I wondered if the pump could cope with a major cold snap.

Being a Green, Kristoffer asked a number of questions and gave me lots of good advice. He'd once had a similar boiler, and besides, he knew a plumber whom he might be able to ask to come by and have a look—if I was interested, of course. Kristoffer and I chatted for a while, and I became increasingly puzzled about why he had actually called me.

He asked me where I lived. I gave him the address, and he promised to write it down and give it to his plumber friend. Then, as a kind of "by the way," he asked me if I had any plans to go into town that day. I lived about twenty-five miles from the office and hadn't intended to go to work that Sunday. I explained this to Kristoffer.

We chatted a little while longer, and in the end I finally asked him straight out what he really wanted. Then he revealed that he was standing outside the office in his T-shirt because he had accidentally locked himself out when he had popped out to fetch some lunch. I looked at the thermometer. Thirty degrees with light snow. We'd been talking for about fifteen minutes! I got into the car and saved him from freezing to the bone.

Everyone else is more important. A Green never asks for anything.

"I Know Exactly What You Mean."

They say Greens are introverts, that is, that they're active in their inner world. This means that they don't talk just for the sake of talking. When you are quieter than those around you, it's natural that you listen. And Greens will listen. They are interested in you and your ideas.

Unlike Reds, who only listen when there is something to be gained from it, or Yellows, who usually don't listen at all (although they will normally deny this fact), Greens hear what you're actually saying. They have a genuine ear for human problems. They might not offer any suggestions or solutions, but they understand what you've told them. Don't assume that means that they agree with you—but they are good listeners.

So far, you have probably tried to puzzle all the pieces together. Where do the different colors fit in? What kind of job would be best for each of them? These are good questions, even if there are no simple answers. One observation that often arises when I work with these issues in different organizations is that Reds, and Yellows in particular, must be good at retail and selling. This is true for sure. But Greens are often overlooked. We always teach salespeople to talk less and listen more, something Greens already do quite naturally.

Helena was a seller I coached a few years ago. She was Green and very gentle in her ways. Most people didn't understand how she survived in that daunting industry. But I have a theory. She once told me about a time when she met a tough chief executive everyone had tremendous respect for. No one in the entire company had managed to sell anything to him, but after a little coaching from me Helena was determined to have a go. So she arranged a meeting.

They ran into each other in the parking lot at the restaurant where they were to meet for lunch. The stern executive cruised into the lot in a vintage car from the late sixties. Beautiful, shiny, and obviously very special. Helena said the only thing she could think of: Wow!

"Do you like cars?" asked the executive, before they had even greeted each other. Helena nodded. Then he told her about the car, how much he had spent to restore it, the paintwork and alloys, the engine. He showed her what it looked like under the hood. Helena nodded and murmured approval and hoped he wouldn't ask her any questions, since she couldn't tell the difference between a Ford and a Chevrolet. But she didn't interrupt; she just listened. After that it was easy. They sat down, and he asked to see the sales agreement. How did she do it? By doing nothing at all except for one thing—listening. He signed before the food was even served.

Conclusions on Green Behavior

Okay. Do you have any Greens in your family? Highly likely.

Mr. Rogers, Gandhi, Michelle Obama, and Jimmy Carter are some well-known people with elements of Green. And, yes, Jesus. There's a guy who knew how to help others.

7

Blue Behavior

In Pursuit of Perfection

"Why Are We Doing This? What's the Science Behind It?"

The last of the four colors is an interesting fellow. You've probably met him. He doesn't make a fuss about himself, but he does keep tabs on what is happening around him. While a Green will just go with the flow, a Blue has all the right answers. In the background, he analyzes: classifies, evaluates, assesses.

You know you've met a Blue if you visit someone's home and everything is organized in a particular way. Clear labels and names on each hook so that the children will know exactly where to hang up their jackets. Dinner menus, divided into six-week intervals to ensure a balanced diet, stuck on the refrigerator door. If you look at his tools, you'll find that everything has its own spot and nothing is out of place. Why? A Blue DIY guy always puts things back where they belong.

He is also a pessimist, sorry: a realist. He sees errors, and he sees risks. He's the melancholic who closes the circle of behavior.

Reserved, analytical, and detail-oriented are some words you might associate with a Blue.

"Excuse Me, but That's Not Quite Accurate."

We all have a friend like that. Think about it: You're sitting in a restaurant with your friends. You're discussing cats, football, or space rockets. Someone throws out a random comment. It may be your Red friend who claims that the Patriots have been to the Super Bowl eleven times; it can be the Yellow who cheerfully claims that as a child he lived in the same block as Will Smith in West Philly.

Your Blue buddy clears his throat and in a gentle voice says that the Patriots have actually only been to the Super Bowl ten times—with their first appearance after the 1985 season and eight times since 2001—and that Will Smith actually grew up in Wynnefield, which is well north of the block in question and a half-hour walk from the lovely Centennial Arboretum. In addition, without blinking an eye, the good friend adds, "It's interesting to note that in the Super Bowl pregame coin toss, of the past fifty-one games, the outcome has been tails twenty-seven times and heads twenty-four times. And based on past statistics, the winner of the coin toss is slightly less likely to win the game overall."

You just have to give up, boys. This guy simply knows everything. He doesn't make a big deal about it, but his way of presenting facts makes it difficult for you to call them into question. He knows where he found the info and can go fetch the book to prove it.

That's the way it is with Blues. They know how things stand before they open their mouth. They've Googled, read the owner's manual, and checked the dictionary—and afterwards they present a report in full.

But an important thing to note: If the question doesn't come up, it's unlikely that your Blue buddy will say anything on the subject.

He has no need to tell everyone about what he knows. Of course, a Blue doesn't know everything; no one can. But you can usually bank on the fact that what he says is correct.

BLUE people often see themselves as:

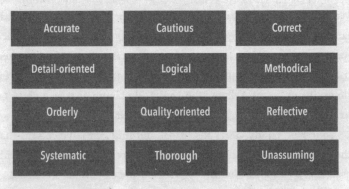

Accurate	Cautious	Correct
Detail-oriented	Logical	Methodical
Orderly	Quality-oriented	Reflective
Systematic	Thorough	Unassuming

Did you notice anything about the art above? Of course you did. This time I listed the different characteristics in alphabetical order—something a Blue would certainly appreciate. However, I might get in trouble because I don't discuss each and every one one of these characteristics individually on the subsequent pages. To all Blue individuals who are reading this—who have probably jotted down a little note in the margin to go to my website to look for possible explanations for this blunder—I just want to say that I didn't mean to cause any strife.

"It's Not a Big Deal—I Was Just Doing My Job."

How can a know-it-all be unassuming? It's impressively modest to avoid making a fuss, even if you know everything.

It's rare that a wholly Blue person would feel the need to stand on the rooftops or to toot his own horn in order to make it clear to the world who the real expert is. It's usually sufficient that you, the Blue, are clear about who knows best.

There are downsides to this modesty. More than once I've stood in the middle of a crowd of people as we all tried to puzzle through a problem together. On one such occasion, a Blue came forward after two hours and casually pointed out the answer. For him, it was never really a problem at all. He knew a thing or two, but because Blues often miss the big picture, they don't always act immediately. I asked him why he didn't say anything two hours earlier. And, like a typical Blue, he said, "Well, you never asked."

It would be easy to feel aggravated by such a comment. But at the same time, I understood him. It's more my problem than his that he wasn't invited to join the discussion. He knew that he knew the answer, and that was good enough.

There's also no need to cheer, applaud, or call a Blue up to the podium when he's done something tremendous in an amazing way. Sure, it doesn't really do any harm to cheer. He'll just nod, accept the praise and the prize check, and then return to his desk, where he'll continue working on the next project. But he may well wonder what the fuss was really all about—he was only doing his job.

"Excuse Me, but Where Did You Read That? And What Edition Was It?"

A Blue can rarely get too many facts or have too many pages of fine print. People say that God is in the details, and I can imagine that it was a Blue who first said that.

No detail is too small to be noticed. Cutting corners is simply not an option for a Blue.

"Hold up," you might say. "Not keeping track of every single tiny detail isn't really the same thing as cutting corners." But if you ask a Blue it is. "Not having full control is the same thing as not having any control at all. What do we get by cutting corners? How can you possibly justify it?"

It doesn't work like that. Tell a Blue that he can ignore the details of the new contract and skip the last thirty paragraphs—there's nothing important in that bit—and he'll stare at you very attentively and wonder about your mental capabilities. As usual, he won't necessarily say anything. He'll just completely ignore what you said. He would rather burn the midnight oil checking all the facts of the case than miss the slightest detail.

A few years ago, I tried to sell a leadership program to the CEO of a company in the packaging industry. He was Blue; there was no doubting that. His emails were long-winded and a little dry, and for our first meeting he had set aside fifty minutes. Not an hour, not three-quarters of an hour, but fifty minutes. (There was a reason for this: After the meeting he would have lunch, and the dining room was eight minutes away. Plus a visit to the gents for about two minutes. A fifty-minute meeting would get him there right in time.)

The first time we met, he deposited me in a specific chair by a specific corner at the visitors' desk. He didn't ask if I had any difficulty getting there—which I did; the address was totally impossible—he offered neither coffee nor tea. He didn't smile when he greeted me. He examined my business card very carefully.

After going through the company's needs, I explained that I would go back to my office to put a quote together. Once back at my desk, I brooded about how I should go about it. Normally, my proposals were ten to twelve pages long, but I knew that wouldn't be sufficient in this case. Instead, I put my nose to the grindstone and wrote over thirty-five pages.

I mailed a hard copy of the quote to him, since for a Blue the written and printed word means much more than the spoken—or digital. After a week or so, I followed the whole thing up with a phone call. They were interesting ideas, the CEO said, but he was ready to go further. Could he now get the full quote? What he actually said was:

"IS THERE ANY MORE MATERIAL?"

I remember scratching my head. In my opinion, I had described the program rather well in the proposal. Each stage had an agenda, a clear goal, and a defined purpose. I'd given some background information, references, and citations.

As a seller, you can't give up, so I was back at it, adding every detail I could think of. The second time, I put together at least eighty-five pages: each item broken down into two-hour intervals, even more background, sample exercises, analysis tools, templates, the works. Details on a level that would have made a Yellow throw up.

Pleased with myself, I sent over the whole caboodle.

It took several weeks before I heard from the CEO. I asked if he was ready to make a decision and he asked:

"IS THERE MORE MATERIAL?"

Well, this time he wanted to come to my office. For ninety minutes, we sat on the same side of the table in the conference room at my office and went through . . . the table of contents in the proposal. He had drawn up the general terms and conditions (read: the fine print) on legal paper, and each section was full of questions and notes. Afterwards, he said with a totally expressionless face that it was the best meeting he had been at for a long time. But what he really wondered was:

"IS THERE ANY MORE MATERIAL?"

I sent him off and sat down for a while and pondered. More material? No problem. I shared the whole training folder (this was before e-learning and virtual classrooms), at least three hundred pages covering every fifteen-minute session during the fifteen days of training in five different stages of leadership.

This was all the material there was, even with information about when coffee breaks should be slotted in, exactly what questions should be asked of the individuals during training, how the room should be furnished, the works. I can certify—there were no gaps.

I thought that if I took all this and rammed it down his throat he would be satisfied at last.

After a month, he asked if there was any more material.

There was not.

A common misconception is that Blues are unable to make decisions, but that's not the case. It wasn't that this CEO was pushing the decision into sometime in the future or that he couldn't decide. He simply had no need to decide. For him, the process leading up to the decision was significantly more interesting. And he just wondered if there was any more material.

Why Some People Have to Sleep on Things for So Long You Wonder If They've Gone into Hibernation

The preceding example also illustrates another important characteristic Blue behavior. They're generally very cautious. They often think safety first. Where a Red or Yellow would take a wild chance, a Blue will hold off and consider everything one more time. There may be more factors to take into account, right? You need to get to the bottom of things before you act.

This can manifest itself in various ways. It's a fact that for the Blue, the trip is more important than the destination, exactly the opposite of a Red. Obviously, this amount of caution can result in no decisions being made at all, and it also means that Blues rarely take any major risks. Never taking any risks ensures a predictable life; we can probably agree on that. I'm not saying anything about how exciting and inspiring it would be; I'm just stating the facts.

Sometimes a Blue can even completely refrain from starting something because he can't assess the risks. I once met a Blue seller who had trained as an engineer. His motto was that the best deal is often the one you didn't make. Risk assessment is a complex thing, and who knows what dangers are lurking out there? A Blue generally solves everything by creating advanced systems that manage the possible risks that may arise. They set three alarm clocks. They leave two hours early when one would be enough. They check and recheck the children's backpacks before school in the morning, even though they packed them the night before and no one has touched the backpacks during the night. They triple-check that the keys are in their pocket and, of course, they are. Where else would they be?

The benefits of this are evident. Blues won't be taken aback by unexpected events in the same way others would be. And in the long run, they save a lot of time.

"It Doesn't Matter If It's Easier. It's Still Not Right."

Things can't be allowed to go wrong. That's all there is to it. Quality is all that matters. When a Blue individual thinks his work runs the risk of being shoddy or low quality, things come to a standstill. Everything must be checked out. Why has the quality declined?

Running the risk of generalizing, I would say that a fair number of engineers have distinct Blue traits. Accurate, systematic, fact oriented, and quality conscious. I can't know for certain, but I would imagine that Toyota, the Japanese car manufacturer, probably has a good proportion of Blue engineers among its employees. They have a policy that you must always ask "why" five times to ensure quality and get to the heart of the issue. I would say that this is a typical Blue approach (in addition to the Japanese mentality, which is very long term and rather Blue in expression).

So let's say someone discovers an oil stain on the floor. A Red approach might be to lambast the person closest to him and then order him to mop up the stain. A Yellow sees the stain and then forgets it but two days later is surprised when he slips on it. The Green also sees the stain and feels a little bit of guilt because it poses a problem and everyone is ignoring it.

A Blue would ask, "Why is there an oil spill?" The answer may be that a gasket is leaking. This answer, of course, is unsatisfactory for a Blue. "Why is the gasket leaking?" "Because it's poor quality." "Why do we have poor-quality gaskets in our factory?" "Because the purchasing department was told to save money. We bought cheap gaskets instead of tight-sealed gaskets." "But who asked us to save money and compromise on quality?" This is the way he goes on. Maybe the problem will resolve itself. Maybe we'll get a report of what went wrong, but nothing is done to fix the problem.

In the end, the Blue solution might be to review our purchasing strategies instead of just mopping up the oil on the floor.

My point is this: A Blue is prepared to dive deep to get everything exactly 100 percent correct.

Blues argue that if they're going to do something, they must do it correctly. And vice versa—if a task isn't worth being done properly, then it's not worth doing at all. Furthermore, because Blues usually find it difficult to lie, they will always point out the defects they uncover—even defects that may reflect poorly on them.

I clearly remember discussions my parents had when I was a child. We moved from time to time, and usually our house had to be sold, with everything that entailed. Dad—the engineer—would, of course, do all the work himself, and he managed the viewings personally.

My mum was always upset that he began each viewing by pointing out all the flaws and shortcomings of the house. It leaked here and there, and some paint had flaked off behind the sofa. "Why are you telling them that?" my mother wondered. "Because this and that is wrong," Dad replied. "Sure, but do you have to tell that to the prospective buyers? Now they may never want to buy the house!"

He didn't understand the problem. As a very honorable and honest person, he couldn't hide the faults he knew were there. He could live with the fact that we rarely made a huge profit on those deals. He'd been honest about the house, because that's how it should be done.

"If the Trail Doesn't Match the Map, There's Something Wrong with the Trail."

Logical and rational thinking is critical to a Blue. Out with all the feelings (as much as possible) and in with logic. Of course, Blues can't turn off their feelings completely—no one can—but they like to say they use rational arguments when making decisions. They value logical thinking highly, but they can very easily become depressed when things don't go their way. And depression has nothing to do with logic and everything to do with feelings.

Few people can repeat the same task an infinite number of times in exactly the same way like Blues can. They have a unique ability to precisely follow instructions to the letter without questioning, provided they understood and approved of it in the beginning.

How do they do this without getting bored or careless? Well, it's logical. If a particular method works, why change it? While a Yellow or Red would find new ways of doing something simply because they were bored, a Blue repeats the same thing time and time again.

Consider how a Blue would put together a piece of furniture from IKEA. If there's a manual, then of course you have to read it thoroughly before you start. Reds, confident that they can easily do this, start screwing and putting together the various parts without even looking to see what's in the rest of the box. Yellows tear up everything, exclaiming that it's going to be great fun to get the furniture in place. They live in the future and can already see a clear picture of the new cabinet on the right wall of the bedroom with Grandma's tablecloth and a lovely vase of tulips on it. They put each part together a little bit haphazardly, without much effort. They'll screw in a few screws where it looks logical only to skip to another part of the cabinet. A Green DIY guy leans the enormous box against the wall and has a coffee break. There really isn't a hurry.

What does a Blue do? He reads the instructions twice, examines what everything looks like, and confirms that the different pieces of the new cabinet match the pictures in the instructions. With a slightly damp—not too wet—cloth, he carefully wipes down all the different parts because they are likely to be dusty. He tallies the number of screws in the box so that he will not be surprised at the end if anything is missing (and if there are any parts left over, he may very well take the whole thing apart again).

It may take a little extra time for a Blue to put together his cabinet, but once it's done, you can be sure that it will stand forever.

"The Devil Is in the Details."

A few years ago, I wanted to renovate the patio in my yard. Because I like working with my hands, in contrast to just talking each day, I thought I would do the job myself. Or at least part of it. My dad, well over seventy at the time, was going to help out because he knew that I was pressed for time.

Easier said than done. To provide a sturdy foundation, we were going to lay down gravel. Dad arrived a few moments before the dump truck with all the gravel. He had his own wheelbarrow with him, specially designed to maneuver gravel, and a special shovel that he always used for similar purposes. He didn't understand why I was standing there with my regular shovel. Everyone knew that you had to use special shovels for things like this.

The truck came and dropped a hefty pile of gravel in the driveway. I imagined a few days of shoveling before me, and to be honest, it made me feel a little tired. But I was still ready to take on the challenge.

My old dad? He picked up a bit of gravel between his fingers, smelled it, felt it, and assessed its quality. After grunting somewhat, which I interpreted as approval, he began to assess the pile itself.

He measured the height of the mound with his hand; he paced how large the circumference was. I asked him what he was doing. He didn't answer but mumbled numbers under his breath.

"One and eighty high, five meters in circumference, gradient . . . hmm . . . " After thirty seconds, he said that there were between 8.75 and 9.25 cubic meters of gravel in the driveway. I confided to him that it was actually nine cubic meters. Exactly.

Dad asked rather skeptically how I knew that. I pointed. "It's written on the truck," I said.

Dad was mildly impressed. I asked if he wanted to count each piece of gravel individually. He didn't deem that to be necessary.

For hours, he walked around the site and packed and pressed, raked the gravel, smoothing everything until he thought that everything was in order. He used a level, plumb line, water, all the means at his disposal, so that nothing would go wrong.

The gravel needed to be laid at an incline of exactly one centimeter per meter. Why, you ask? "It says so in the book." Because he was a construction engineer, he knew the book by heart. One centimeter per meter. Exactly. Who knows what terrible consequences could result if you were careless about that?

Consider the difference between one centimeter and roughly one centimeter. The former is precise; the latter is imprecise. Roughly one centimeter—it could be up two centimeters if things went bad. From a one-centimeter to a two-centimeter gradient—that's a difference of no less than 100 percent, a huge deviation!

(The funny thing about this story is not really the event itself, but what happened when Dad read about it in the first edition of this book. He argued that that's not how it really happened. He corrected the story on several points and claimed that the truck had held twelve cubic meters—not nine. He also insists that he's not purely Blue, and there might just be something in that.)

He's like that with everything. At home, if there are any technical questions about a television, a car, a microwave oven, or a cell phone, out comes the manual. He always replies, "It says here that. . . Why do you think they wrote this stuff if it's not meant to be done that way?"

How do you reply to that? How do you argue with the instruction manual? It's impossible to find arguments that a true Blue will accept. (My dad will also stop at a red light in the middle of the night, even if he is the only one within a ten-mile radius. Because that's the way you do it.)

The great value of this approach is obvious. He will never be fooled; he will always get what he paid for. It gives him an inner peace because he knows he has checked everything out very accurately.

If you know any Blues, I am sure you will agree with me. Under normal circumstances, they're very calm and balanced. Probably because they keep tabs on everything.

"Silence Is Golden."

Introvert. Enough said. I could stop there. Many Blues I've met don't say a single word unnecessarily. That's just the way it is. Does that mean they have nothing to say? Don't they have opinions about things? Not at all, they are just very, very introverted. Blues are the calm, stable individuals the Aztecs equated with the sea, the element of water.

Quiet on the outside, but under the surface anything could be happening. "Introverted" doesn't mean silent; it means active in the inner world. But the effect of this is often quiet.

In general, my advice is to listen attentively when Blues do actually talk, because they've usually thought through what they say.

So why are they so silent? Among other things, it's because they, unlike Yellows, don't feel the need to be heard. Sitting in a corner and not being seen or heard makes no difference to them. They are observers, spectators, more than central characters. They can find themselves at the edge of a group where they observe and record everything that is said.

And don't forget this: According to a Blue's values, being silent is something positive. If you have nothing to say—keep quiet.

Conclusions on Blue Behavior

Do you know everything about Blues? Have you identified some Blues in your life? Bill Gates and Albert Einstein both used their attention to detail and meticulous nature to build their success. We also have Sandra Day O'Connor and Condoleezza Rice. And of course, from the fictional world, Mr. Spock from *Star Trek* is the perfect Blue—all logic, rationality, and intellect, even if a few of the jokes slip past him.

8

No One Is Completely Perfect

Strengths and Weaknesses

As the title of this book suggests, there are individuals around us who, under less favorable circumstances, we may find challenging to understand. There are others we don't understand at all, no matter what the situation is. And the most difficult to interact with are those who aren't like us, because they obviously behave "incorrectly."

The Differences Begin to Become Clear

You can see the general differences among the different colors. The illustration on page 63 shows an example of how they differ. Some people are issue-oriented, and others are relation oriented. While two of them (Red and Yellow) are quick to act, the Greens and Blues are reflective. This is often the source of everyday misunderstandings, both large and small. I will come back to this on page 193, but I would like to take this opportunity to provide some nuances to the illustration of the different core behavior patterns that each color represents.

I'm not saying that you would call people idiots, like Sture, who opened my eyes at the beginning of this book. However, in all hon-

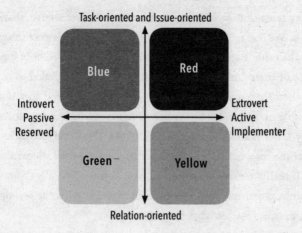

esty, all of us, on occasion, have just stood there, unable to comprehend a comment we've heard or watched someone behave in way that is diametrically opposed to how we would have behaved. And so we believe that they're idiots.

This reasoning assumes that "I am always right," which of course means that the other person, and their form of behavior, is automatically wrong. It's a tricky question. A wise person once said that "just because you're right, I don't have to be wrong." We also tend to pay special attention to the faults and shortcomings of others. Child psychologists have argued that the things we find most shocking in the behavior of our children are the things we recognize in ourselves—but wish we didn't do. So who decides what kind of behavior is right and wrong?

Time for a Real Cliché

On the one hand, no one is perfect. There you go, a real platitude. But really, there are no perfect human beings; no one is without faults or shortcomings. In my youth, I was constantly looking for a role model who could become my mentor in life—that person, a man or woman, completely free from shortcomings—but I never found one. I still haven't seen any trace of this elusive perfect human. And, of course, that's the way it is. We live with our shortcomings and make the best of things.

On the other hand, when we think someone is an idiot is it really because of their faults and shortcomings or have we failed to understand them? An attribute that may be useful in some situations is unsuitable in others. It's important to remember that communication usually takes place on the recipient's terms. Whatever people's judgment of me may be, that is the way they perceive me. Regardless of what I really meant or intended. As always, it's all about self-awareness. Good qualities can become drawbacks in the wrong circumstances, no matter what the quality is.

Quick Review of Core Behavior Patterns

Reds are quick and more than happy to take command if needed. They make things happen. However, when they get going, they become control freaks and can be hopeless to deal with. And they repeatedly trample on people's toes.

Yellows can be amusing, creative, and elevate the mood regardless of who they're with. However, when they are given unlimited space, they will consume all the oxygen in the room, they won't allow anyone into a conversation, and their stories will reflect reality less and less.

The friendly **Greens** are easy to hang out with because they are so pleasant and genuinely care for others. Unfortunately, they can be too wishy-washy and unclear. Anyone who never takes a stand eventually becomes difficult to handle. You don't know where they really stand, and indecision kills the energy in other people.

The analytical **Blues** are calm, levelheaded, and think before they speak. Their ability to keep a cool head is undoubtedly an enviable quality for all who aren't capable of doing that. However, Blues' critical thinking can easily turn to suspicion and questioning those around them. Everything can become suspect and sinister.

In the following sections, I deal with how people might perceive the weaknesses of certain behavior patterns. Naturally, this is a sensitive area and can be easily misunderstood. When I coach individuals, this is usually where things can get messy. So as you read on be aware that much is in the eye of the beholder. Who is right and who is wrong? The behavior patterns I am talking about are described as other people may perceive them, even if the intention of the person who just made a fool of himself might have been completely different.

One thing I know for sure regarding the different colors is that each color evaluates themselves in different ways. Reds and Yellows tend to inflate their strengths and believe that they have no weaknesses. They have powerful egos, and a great part of their success can probably be attributed to the fact that they don't get bogged down in faults and shortcomings but instead look for opportunities and good news. Clearly, this can't be maintained over time.

Conversely, Greens and Blues usually exaggerate their weaknesses and in certain cases even ignore their strengths. The consequences are clear. When you give positive feedback to a Green or a Blue, they sometimes appear to be immune to it and change the subject to something that went seriously wrong. Obviously, this is highly unproductive.

Well—are we ready to go?

How Red People Are Perceived

If you ask other people about Reds, you might get a different picture from the one the Red gives of himself. What a surprise! My own private research shows that Reds are surrounded by more idiots than the rest of us. Many people will agree with what you have read up to now about Reds, but I have also heard other comments. Usually, they express this when the Red is not in the room because they are afraid of his fiery temper. You've heard him say that he wants to hear the truth. Over the years, he's bellowed into our ears "Say what you think!" But as soon as you do, you find yourself in the middle of a heated discussion with an angry Red. This means that what you are going to read now will often be completely new for many Reds. Not many of us have ever been able to make these points to a Red before. It takes way too much energy.

Some people say that Reds are just belligerent, arrogant, and egotistical. They are perceived as unyielding, impatient, aggressive, and controlling.

I don't think this is necessarily correct, but I've even heard people speak about people with Red behavior as dictatorial and tyrannical. Suddenly the picture isn't as flattering. The born leader reveals his blemished side.

First of all, let me say this: Nothing said previously would necessarily bother a Red, because he is more task oriented than relationship oriented. Besides, everyone else is wrong. But let's see what everyone else has to say.

"Why Does Everything Take So Long? Can't You Speed Things Up a Bit?"

Well, what can you say? A person willing to step outside any regulatory framework to get ahead is nothing if not impatient. When the usual official channels take too long, a Red will scale over a few levels of decision makers and expeditiously look for the person who really calls the shots.

The first example that comes to mind was the traffic in my beautiful capital city. Sure, many locals are in more of a hurry than the national average when they sit behind the wheel—there are statistics about this. But since we're talking about Red behavior, I'd like to tell you about a colleague I had a few years ago. Björn and I used a car as our principal means of transport in and around the city. It simply took too long to use public transport. Björn lost his license every so often because of his somewhat liberal approach to speed limits.

He lived far outside the city, and the journey into the office, about twenty miles away, could take about forty minutes. That was on a good day; it could just as easily take an hour and a half.

Björn rarely felt the need to adjust his driving according to the flow of traffic. His opinion was that there was no reason for him to follow every single traffic rule. The posted speed limits here and there—fifty, sixty, and so on—they were mostly recommendations. They didn't apply to him. They were there for people who didn't really know how to drive a car!

On one occasion I was sitting in the office with a few colleagues having a cup of coffee, discussing the rather serious traffic situation. It felt as if the city was on the verge of a traffic infarction. Björn didn't know what we were talking about. He wasn't aware of the problem at all. On the contrary, he felt that the traffic hadn't been bad lately. When we questioned him a bit more, it turned out that he usually drove in the bus lane. All the way. For over twenty miles. It was so much quicker that way. Björn even maintained that this was okay. You could even get a permit for the bus lane. That's what he did, and it cost him about $140 a month.

About every four weeks the police stopped him, but it was worth it. Just imagine how much time he saved! And all it cost him was the fines. He felt it was a good deal.

This story illustrates quite clearly how Red behavior works. They know just as well as everyone else that it's wrong to break the rules; however, since it's quicker that way, they do it anyway. Reds are notorious rule breakers. Once again, I would like to remind you of their intentions—to get the job done.

Reds have no problem taking one or two shortcuts, as long as it's about getting things done. With such a generous approach to regulations and rules, you'll definitely arrive faster. I would even say that a Red is often so fast that if something were to go wrong he would still manage to redo the project. At the same time, no one else ever really knows what's going to happen.

"I Am Not Screaming! *I'm Not Angry! Aaarrrghhhh!*"

Because the way Reds communicate is so blunt and so direct, many perceive them as aggressive. This is logical, but at the same time this perception varies, depending on who becomes the victim of the Red's forceful points of view. For instance, in Sweden it's not acceptable to behave in the kind of confrontational manner that would be fine in Germany or France. I'm not saying that people quarrel more in these countries, but that they have a slightly different approach to conflicts.

Just imagine. In many workplaces people are encouraged to be candid and "have open communication." What does this really mean? It's easy to interpret it as meaning we should all be honest with one another and just say whatever we think, right? We want to have open and forthright dialogue. That's excellent; for any organization to be efficient, it's necessary to have straightforward communication about things that are important.

So who excels at frank communication? And can receive the same without getting cranky? Answer: No one.

Besides Reds, of course. For them, this is a nonissue. "Why are we even talking about communication? It's obvious that you say what you think!" Many people find this stressful; to constantly have the truth pushed into your face can be onerous if you have difficulty taking it.

My goal here isn't to define what's right or wrong; I only want to establish that all of us are different.

So why do we sometimes perceive Red behavior as threatening and belligerent? Could it be that they don't give up right away? That they like to argue and debate even small matters if they find them important? That they'll raise their voices, glare daggers at people, and pound their fists on the table if it suits them? That sometimes they express themselves rather rudely?

Imagine the following scenario:

You have a project, something that you've spent a few days on, or maybe even weeks. You begin to doubt yourself—have you succeeded at your work? Is it as good as you wanted it to be? Would you dare show it to the client as it is now, or should you ask for some feedback from someone who you know will give you an honest answer?

Just then a Red comes sauntering by, and you take a chance. You are fully aware that this colleague—spouse, friend, cousin, neighbor—will be honest. You ask for a frank opinion. With a degree of pride in your voice, you show him what you've accomplished, and you go through your process step by step. Without you noticing, the Red becomes impatient because he's already decided what his opinion is and he's getting tired of you doing all the talking for so long.

With a wave of his hand that effectively silences you, the Red says, "It doesn't look that good. I don't really like what you've done here. In fact, it looks pretty rough. I'm amazed that you didn't do better than this. I think you have to redo the whole thing from start to finish."

Then he leaves without thinking any more about it. You're left there feeling forlorn and crushed, regardless of what color you are.

Exaggerated? Can this happen in real life? At this stage, if you believe that such nasty people don't really exist then you've never met a genuine Red. Or the Reds you have met have essentially learned how to be dishonest.

Think about it. What's the purpose of cutting a person down to size so completely? What were the Red's intentions? It was to do exactly what you asked. You wanted an honest opinion!

"Say exactly what you think," you said. It's possible you even added: "I won't be angry/ sad/disappointed/suicidal." "Be prepared," says the Red, "because here it comes." By asking for an honest opinion, you released a flood of brutal candor. But you'll survive—perhaps with your self-confidence a little waterlogged and your ego utterly drowned.

As a consultant, I have explained countless times that when a Red goes all out on an issue that's important to him, an issue on which he does not intend to give up—well, the storm will be brutal. If you're afraid of conflict, then you shouldn't put yourself in that situation. A Red has no problem with conflict. Reds don't consciously create conflict, but a refreshing quarrel every now and then can be a good thing, don't you think? It's just another way to communicate.

A little tip: The worst thing you can do once you get into a conflict with a Red is back off. That tactic can cause you serious problems. More on that later.

"What Are You Doing over There? I Can See What You're (Not) Doing!"

What's behind the need to control? Simply put, the desire for control is a phenomenon where an individual needs to have power over a situation in which either groups or individuals are present. Those who have control needs often feel extremely uneasy about having to adapt themselves to a group or a situation and will eagerly come up with various strategies to avoid this. A common form of behavior is to talk constantly, interrupting and ignoring others, in order to maintain control over the conversation.

Reds can probably be perceived as extremely overbearing, but it's important to note they are interested in controlling those around them, but not in controlling every specific detail of a situation. (Attention to or control over detail isn't something we can accuse Reds of.) But it is important for a Red to feel that he can influence what people do and how they intend to act on certain specific issues.

At the heart of this need for control is a belief that they know more than anyone else. And because a Red feels he knows best, he will keep tabs on everyone around him to ensure that they all do the right thing. The advantage for a Red is that he gets everything done his way. The disadvantage is obvious: everyone else feels controlled. Some people think it's a good thing when someone else makes the decisions and holds the baton, but others feel limited and just want to escape.

Many years ago, I worked for a company in which one of the middle managers was quite Red. (She was also a bit Blue—see the section on Blue behavior.) When she delegated tasks to the employees the effect was quite amusing. She usually had no problem relinquishing certain things; she was even good at delegating enjoyable tasks, something many executives can find difficult. However, since she was Red, she was very quick in thought and action. In practice, this meant that she hung around after she had delegated a specific task—and if the task wasn't done immediately she would simply go and do it herself. When the employee in question got to that item on his to-do list, he often discovered that it had already been done. Note: The deadline hadn't been reached yet.

Because this middle manager was Red-Blue, she did a much better job than what the employee would have had he been given the chance. Red means fast; Blue means high quality in implementation. Unfortunately, criticism of the employee's sluggishness was not slow in coming. As the Blue part of this manager was precise with the details and the Red part gave criticism very readily, she was perceived as quite rigid. Which brings us on to the next section.

"I Try to Care About You, but It Would Help If You Were a Little More Interesting."

Have you ever met a person completely without feelings? No, I thought so. Once again—Reds are not typical relational people. Nothing wrong with that, as long as the person you are communicating with has the same focus as you. But if a Red speaks to a pronounced relational person, like a Yellow or a Green, he can be perceived as very coldhearted or inhuman.

Let me illustrate this with an example from my own personal experience.

I had a colleague, whom I always appreciated very much (notice that I start with the positives, to avoid ruffling feathers—very Swedish of me) and still have great respect for as a professional but also as a good friend. Okay, it's the infamous Björn again.

A few years ago, we were having a tough period in the company. Fall had been a difficult and strenuous time: long days, late nights, and frequent weekend work. We had worn ourselves out, we had worn one another out, and we had worn out our respective families. We were on our knees. We really deserved a quiet and restful holiday season.

For the company holiday party we went to a Japanese restaurant. We had taken our shoes off and were sitting on cushions, each holding a glass of sake in his hands. In typical Swedish fashion, we looked at the menus while, at the same time, keeping an eye on what the others were thinking of ordering. Of course, most of us didn't want to order something that no one else chose.

Except for Björn. He glanced quickly through the menu and declared what he had in mind. He was ready now and quickly grew weary of those of us who hadn't decided yet. Needing something to do, he started a conversation. At the time, my daughter had just changed schools, and Björn was inquisitive.

"How did everything go with the new school? How's the little lassie doing?" Pleasantly surprised by his concern for my daughter, I started to tell him. After about twenty seconds I noted that Björn's eyes began to wander. He looked around the restaurant with a facial expression that said: Why is he telling me this?

He looked at me with a smile I interpreted as You know me. You know how I function. I don't actually want to talk any more about that! And he quickly began talking about something completely different.

Ordinarily, I should have been a little bit offended, maybe even insulted. How can anyone be so insensitive? Especially when the other person is talking about something that he himself inquired about?

Does this mean that Björn is coldhearted or that he cares nothing for other people? Not at all. He cares just as much as anyone else, but when he realized that everything was fine with my daughter he simply lost interest. In usual fashion, he announced that the channel of communication was closed. Instead of sitting there hemming and hawing, pretending to be interested in more or less meaningless details, he said exactly what he felt.

Remember that we're talking about interpretations and perceptions here. The intention behind a particular behavior is one thing; how we as recipients perceive it is another. Personally, I just wanted to laugh the whole thing off, because I knew Björn very well. I knew that he would never dream of hurting anyone deliberately. When he tramples on people's toes from time to time it's never intentional—it just happens. In reality, he is one of the warmest and most generous people I have ever met. It's just that you have to know him to understand this.

What would have been the correct answer to Bjorn's question about my daughter?

"Great."

It would have been enough.

"It Takes Strength to Be Alone, and I'm the Strongest of You All."

The word "egotistic" comes from the Latin word *"ego,"* meaning "I." My I is, therefore, my ego. Linguistically, we have consequently chosen to put some kind of equal sign between people with strong egos and being selfish. Naturally, there are many people in our world who are selfish and egotistical. The world is teeming with them. Again, I want you to remember that we are speaking here about perceived behavior.

If we look at how a Red communicates, we can understand why many perceive him as egotistic:

- "I think we should accept this proposal."
- "I want that assignment."
- "This is what I think about it."
- "I have a good idea."
- "Will we do this my way or the wrong way?"

Add a sharp eye and distinctive body language and you will see someone who will take what he wants. He will fight for his interests. He will tell everyone who will listen that he is capable of doing whatever he undertakes. Some people, especially Greens, find that this "I" form of speaking is unsettling. A Red's "I" message occupies their minds. (They share this trait with Yellows, who also have strong egos.)

But we've learned to take care of one another. We know that being solitary is not the same thing as being strong, that we need one another to survive. Cooperation is the model, and I've preached this for over two decades. So we think it's egotistic when Reds speak only about themselves. They make sure to help themselves before helping others. They are often willing to trample on someone else if they see an opportunity to advance themselves. They may not do this consciously, but the effect is the same.

Reds often come out the winners in discussions. They see this as a natural part of a conversation. They always know best and will assert that everyone else is wrong. It suits their ego to behave this way. The aftermath of this method is that they lose friends, people can dislike them, and they are cut off from information because no one wants them in the group. Once they've noticed this, they may well just decide that all the other people are idiots.

A few years ago, I was one of six people who was seated at the table having an evening meal. In some anguish, a man, Green-Blue, told me he was not feeling well. He couldn't live up to the responsibilities his employer laid on his shoulders. He was hard-pressed by his burdensome workload, and he found it difficult to sleep at night. This caused even more stress for him because he knew that if he didn't get a good night's rest it would be even harder for him to perform at work. His wife, sitting beside him, tried to hide her discomfort. The situation was certainly not comfortable for anyone in the room. Everyone at the table offered encouraging remarks along with cautious questions about how he thought he might be able to reverse the difficult situation. We all expressed our support as far as we could.

Except for the Red. After ten minutes, the only Red at the table finally had enough and tore into the distraught, stressed-out little devil.

The Red's analysis was as clear as day: "I think you complain too much. You're just earning your salary. I've never been sick, and I think people worry too much; I would never end up in your situation, and I really think you should pull yourself together."

What a dinner that was! Let's be honest—Reds are the ones who always believe they are surrounded by idiots.

How Yellow People Are Perceived

Funny, entertaining, and almost divinely positive. Absolutely. Again—this is their own interpretation. If you ask other people about Yellows, you may well get a somewhat different picture. Many people will agree with what you have read up to now, but you will also hear other comments. It's especially fun to ask the Blues. They will say that Yellows are selfish, superficial, and overly self-confident. Someone else will say that they talk too much and are bad listeners. Combine that with the observation that they can be distracted and careless. Suddenly the picture is not as flattering.

When a Yellow hears these comments, one of two things can happen. Either he gets deeply distressed and genuinely hurt, or he sets off a ferocious argument. It depends. What's striking is that, over time, none of this criticism will really torment a Yellow very much. On the one hand, he's a bad listener, and on the other hand, he has what some psychologists might call a selective memory. He simply forgets the difficult bits, and with his positive ethos he finds it easy to say to himself that he doesn't have any faults or shortcomings.

Let's have a look at what Yellows struggle with—even if they don't always know it.

"Hello, Anyone There? Listen to What Happened to Me! You Want to Know, Right?"

At the beginning of this chapter, I pointed out that Yellows are very good communicators. I would like to repeat that now.

Yellows are *very* good communicators. With an emphasis on "very." None of the other colors come close to the Yellows' ease in finding words, expressing themselves, and telling a story. It comes so easily, so simply, so effortlessly, that you can't help being impressed. It's common knowledge that most people don't like speaking in front of others. They get heart palpitations and sweaty palms, terrified of making fools of themselves. This is totally alien to Yellows. Making fools of themselves isn't part of the deal, and if the improbable were to happen you could always laugh it off with another amusing anecdote.

However, it may be too much of a good thing. Regardless of what you are good at, there is a limit, a time to break off. Yellows, especially those without self-awareness, don't have such a limit. It would never even occur to them to wrap up; if they have something to say, out it comes. The fact that no one else thinks it's important is neither here nor there.

A Yellow behaves exactly like most people—he does what he's good at. And he is good at talking. There are countless examples of Yellows who completely dominate a conversation. Then add a hefty dose of poor listening and an interesting (read: one-sided) communication takes place.

Many people become hugely frustrated by this limitless verbosity. It's often perceived as egocentrism. The terms "windbag," "verbal diarrhea," and "motormouth" were more than likely coined with Yellows in mind.

Countless times I've experienced the following: A group of people are sitting around a boardroom table. The top dog in the room expresses an idea; it can be about anything at all. When the time comes for comments, all the Yellows will reinforce the idea by repeating the exact same thing, possibly with their own words. (I would like to say to the women reading this that I am aware of the fact that this is more male behavior than female.) Why do they do that? Well, first, it's important to signal when you are in agreement, and second, they can say it so much better.

A few years ago, I was with a management team studying group dynamics. I had just purchased a cell phone with a stopwatch. Using this, I could time who had spoken in the group and for how long.

In the room were the CEO and his seven closest associates. Peter, the sales manager, was really Yellow and he had only had one point of the nineteen on the agenda. Take a good look at the ratio 1:19. This represents around 5.3 percent of the agenda.

The CEO opened the meeting, but pretty soon a clear pattern emerged. Peter had opinions about every single item on the agenda. I used my stopwatch and was fascinated by what I saw. He spoke 69 percent of the time. Yes. It's true. Thirty-one percent went to the other seven, including the CEO himself.

If you're Yellow, you may have already charged on ahead in this book, because you possibly recognized yourself and thought that this was a very unfair example. Everyone else is wondering how that's even possible. How can one person dominate the conversation so fully? It's possible because Yellows have no problems delivering opinions, views, and advice regardless of whether they know anything about the subject or not. A Yellow has a generous approach to his own ability—when an idea pops up in his head, he simply opens his mouth.

People say that for Reds thought and action are the same thing. For Yellows, I would suggest the idea that thought and speech are interrelated. What Yellows share is often completely unprocessed material that just tumbles out of the big opening on their faces. Sure, it might be well thought out, but it's usually not. What's most deceptive is that, almost without exception, it sounds very good. Yellows know a thing or two about presenting an idea so that it always sounds fantastic. If you're unfamiliar with this particular person, you may very well take everything he says as true—a serious mistake.

Very often a Yellow is both entertaining and inspiring, and as I said, they can inspire people to new ideas. But should you get into a conversation with a Yellow, you need to be observant so that when he catches his breath you can quickly insert a comment. Or simply close the meeting.

"I Know It Looks Messy, but There's a Method to the Madness!"

A Yellow would hardly admit that he's careless. But he has no natural way to keep track of things. He finds working in a structured way boring. Then you have to fit the mold and follow the template. If there is anything that Yellows avoid, it's feeling controlled by fixed systems.

The solution is to keep everything in your head, which doesn't work. It's not possible to remember everything. So inevitably the Yellow forgets and those around him think he's careless. Missed appointments, forgotten deadlines, and half-finished projects all because once his mind has finished the task he doesn't go backwards. He goes forward. Leaps to the next project. Deals with other things.

Details. To complete a project, you usually need to be precise about details. Yellows don't like keeping track of details. I would even venture to say that they're not interested in details. They paint with broad strokes.

Generally, Yellows are very good at launching things. They're resourceful, and with boundless creativity at their disposal, they can kick off various kinds of projects. But they're not as good at finishing things. Finishing anything 100 percent requires an ability to concentrate that a Yellow rarely possesses. He gets tired and moves on. And so we think that he's careless. He thinks that his work is good enough. My goodness, why worry about trifles? This turned out quite well, after all! The fact that threads are hanging from the shirt or that the document is full of spelling errors is not as important as thinking up new things.

This is repeated in many different spheres. I have a few acquaintances who are hopeless at keeping time. They are always pleased and excited to think things up, but they are optimists when it comes to time. It makes absolutely no difference what time you suggest; they will not be on time. Seven o'clock, half past seven, or eight. It's unimportant. They're late regardless. And when they talk about it, they haggle down their late arrival from forty-five minutes to a little over fifteen minutes. After a while, they actually believe it themselves. But it doesn't matter—the rest of us wait patiently because their presence will be the highlight of the evening.

"Look, I Can Juggle All the Balls at the Same Time!"

We need to talk a little about Yellow's inability to concentrate. He's always prepared for new experiences. This is the downside to the incredible openness Yellows have for new things, ideas, and impressions. There are so many new things!

And because "new" is synonymous with "good" for a Yellow, it's best that something new happens all the time. Otherwise, our Yellow friend will lose focus. He can't be bothered listening to the whole story, the background, and all the details and facts that may actually be relevant. It's not interesting to him, and he will lose his concentration.

What does he do then? Simple. Something else. He throws up another ball to juggle. The problem with all these balls is that he might be able to keep them in the air for a while, but he can't get them down into the right box at the right time. Instead, he leaves the room and the juggled balls tumble down right into someone else's lap. In a meeting, he may very well start playing with his mobile phone or his computer or will start chatting to the person beside him. Softly at first, thinking that no one will notice anything. It's not true, of course; everyone gets quite irritated. But if no one says anything he'll just continue. Here Yellows are like little children. They are good at testing the limits. They continue until someone becomes too angry and puts his foot down. And, of course, then the Yellow feels hurt. He just wanted to . . .

The way Yellows often quickly get bored can have far greater consequences than a little disruptive behavior during meetings. They're not good at everyday trivial things like administration and follow-ups. As usual, most Yellows would contest what I just wrote. In their own eyes, they are the masters even here. But if we consider the ability to follow up, this could be a serious threat to the effective implementation of a project.

New project—great! Put together a new and dynamic team full of interesting people—check! Get everything going and develop ideas and concepts—are you kidding? Already done that! Working like crazy in the beginning to really get things sped up? Yup. But then? Following up on what is actually happening or not happening in a project is extremely boring. That means looking backwards; that's dull, and it won't happen. A Yellow can't keep his concentration long enough to follow through. He would rather persuade himself that it's important to have confidence in people and just trust that the project gets done

A funny example happened once when I coached sales reps at a large commercial TV channel. I sat with a female seller, a clever young woman who made big business deals. We had identified some weaknesses in her behavior profile—after she had struggled to convince me that even bad traits could be quite good—and now started to make a plan for how she would proceed in her personal development.

It began to fall apart on the first point: When would she begin?

She couldn't start that day because it was already past three in the afternoon. And tomorrow was full of meetings. It had to be next week. But she was away then. Maybe the week after that; she would check her calendar and see.

She had lost the match before she had even begun.

"Me! Me!! Me!!!"

Yellows aren't necessarily more selfish than others, but they always seem to be. Why? Mostly because of their dialogue, since they primarily talk about themselves. And when other people are not sufficiently interesting and exciting, a Yellow will interrupt and guide the topic towards something far more interesting—not infrequently himself.

I remember a seller I encountered during a conference with a pharmaceutical company a few years ago. Gustav exhibited all of the less successful aspects of Yellow behavior, and the problem was that he was completely unaware of it. He very rarely spoke about anything but himself and the things he had done, and he behaved as if he were the one who was leading the conference and not me. I have my methods to deal with those boys. But it's amusing to study them for a while before I adjust their behavior with a few choice words during the first break.

A few examples: Every time I put a question to the group, Gustav answered. His quick answers would have indicated engagement—if it had not been for the fact that he was often actually spewing nonsense. He simply said the things that popped into his head. He couldn't keep his thoughts in his own head, and everything just tumbled out. When I directed my attention to one of Gustav's colleagues instead of him, he simply leaned into my field of vision and continued talking.

When I began directing questions to specific people in the room—simply calling them by name—Gustav answered anyway. Pretty impressive, right? He would speak for a while and then ask Sven, "That's what you were going to say, right, Sven?" Sven just shook his head. He was used to this. Gustav continued like that the whole morning before I could rein in him. He just charged in whenever there was a gap or a few seconds' silence.

He never allowed anyone to speak and everything he said was to be taken as gospel truth. He dominated the room without even thinking about the other nineteen people. The funny thing was that everyone was aware of what was going on. But no one had the energy to stand up to Gustav. They just stared at me with slight desperation in their eyes, hoping that I had some way of silencing him.

During lunch, he proclaimed far and wide, so that everyone heard it, that he thought the conference was going very well. By that point the majority of the group hated the very sound of his voice. They could barely put up with him. To save them from their suffering, I had to have a quick feedback intervention with him during the coffee break—something you'll learn more about when I discuss giving feedback.

"You Never Told Me That, I Would Remember!"

If a Yellow is anything, it's a bad listener. They're really miserable at it, in point of fact. Many Yellows I have met say that they are very good listeners—and of course supplied entertaining examples of this undeniable fact—but maybe it could be their memory that was at fault. Basically, they believe that they listen very well, but somewhere along the way to the brain's storage shelves whatever they heard simply gets lost—poof!

No, it's not about memory. It's about how a Yellow is often uninterested in what others say because he knows he could say it so much better himself. He doesn't stay focused; he begins thinking about other things, begins doing other things. He does not want to listen—he wants to talk.

They're also quite childish in that they only like doing things that are enjoyable. If a statement or story or just a normal conversation is boring, then they close their ears. Of course, there's a remedy—take a course in entertaining rhetoric; then you may be able to keep your Yellow friend's, partner's, or colleague's attention. If you can present your message in a more amusing way, he'll at least remain seated a bit longer. Rhetoric isn't the art of talking but rather the art of getting others to listen.

If you have a good friend whom at this stage you have identified as Yellow, you know exactly what I'm talking about. In mid-sentence, he opens his mouth and starts talking about something completely different. Bad memory? No, you were simply being tedious. But truly—add a bad memory into the equation and we really are in trouble.

Many truly successful people in society are often better listeners than the general average. They don't willingly talk as much as they listen. They already know what they know, and to learn more they simply have to hush up and hear what others are saying. It's a way to absorb new knowledge. This is something Yellows need to understand better if they're not to be perceived as completely hopeless—or just stagnant in their personal development. They must, for example, listen to the message I have presented in this last section. If they refuse to take it in just because it is a difficult and possibly a boring message, they'll never learn anything.

How Green People Are Perceived

So what do others—other colors—think about Greens? The picture is ambivalent. Besides the fact that they are considered pleasant, friendly, and caring, there are other opinions. A person who, out of fear of conflict, says yes but means no—how do you handle him? How do you know what he really thinks?

Reds and Yellows especially have problems with what I call the silent resistance. Remaining silent rather than speaking out. Certain Greens, however, tend to tell the truth behind the back of the person concerned. Therefore, others can perceive a Green as dishonest, even though their intention is only to avoid conflict. In general, Greens always expect the worst and therefore tend to lie low.

Then we have the Green's inability to change. When a Green understands the need for change but still says no thanks, that leads those closest to him to think that he is afraid of change, stubborn, unconcerned, and indifferent. As usual, we are talking about perceptions. If we ask Reds what they think about Greens, there will be some heavy opinions.

Pigheadedness Will Never Be a Virtue

What do you do with a person who never changes his views? Ever? Not even when the facts indicate that it's time to take a different path? How do you handle someone whose resolve to continue on the present course has completely taken over?

The difference between Greens and Blues is that while a Blue holds out for more facts about an issue, Greens expect everything to simply blow over, since they refuse to change their minds. They've made a decision about something and will not concede. Why? Because they don't usually do that.

Think about it: It may have taken you your whole life to come to a particular opinion about the dangerous cholesterol in food, about space travel, or about Britney Spears. Suddenly this guy comes along and says that you should exchange your current opinion for his.

It's not going to happen. The Green is waiting for the right feeling to come over him before he makes any changes. If it doesn't, well . . . they're often rather patient.

Let me tell you about a young man, the son in a family I've known very well for many years. This guy is reasonably good in school; his grades are okay. He has many pals.

At the outset, I would like to point out that when we speak about young people, in this case a teenager, we must be careful. This isn't a fully developed behavior profile or character. Young people still have things to learn about life in general. All impressions are not definitive.

So what's the problem?

This young man has his own ideas about what is true and false. And wild horses couldn't get him to change his mind. It may be something he heard from a friend or something he saw on television or something he picked up in school. When this knowledge or idea, irrespective of its source, has been established in his consciousness, it can't be dislodged. It makes no difference how often his parents point out the facts or how tough they are when they present the evidence—his point of view is clear. It doesn't even matter if they point out the danger in this or that way of thinking; he persists in his belief.

Think about it. You supply all the available facts, and the guy says that he understands. He agrees that it sounds logical. Other people could feasibly do it that way, with good results. But still, he's not prepared to change his point of view. Some people would call this pigheadedness.

What's the reason for this? Excellent question. It may be a result of where he first got the information. If a friend says that you can earn just as much money collecting trash as a newly qualified doctor can earn, it doesn't really matter if it's true or not. If the same friend suggests that you can't be arrested for drunk driving if you drive your car after drinking three beers, then this becomes the truth, even if we, with all the facts at our disposal, know that this is simply not the case.

If this guy is told that he'll get a terrific job if he just works a little harder at mathematics, it becomes true. If he got this info from his best mate, it simply has to be true. If a Green trusts in a particular individual, that individual's word becomes law. This makes it easy to exploit Greens, because they can be a little naïve and gullible. And unfortunately, certain people take advantage of this fact.

Sometimes this obstinacy becomes a strength, no doubt about that. But when those around them perceive it as pure pigheadedness, it can create problems.

"Why Bother? Nothing Is Worth Caring About."

Since Greens rarely make the first move and almost always allow others to step up first, you can easily get the impression that a Green is not especially interested or engaged. And often that's the case. He is more passive than he is active, and this has an impact on his behavior. Not much is going on there.

And what does it really matter? If you stay at home—nothing can really go wrong then, right? What Greens fail to see is that most other people want to do things. They assume that everyone thinks as they do and stays on the sofa. They are satisfied with doing nothing. Anything that upsets this standpoint becomes a threat. The result? Even more passivity.

On one occasion, I heard a Red-Yellow boss describe his employees as uninspired and uninterested in their work. It tormented him because no matter how hard he tried to entice and insist, they never left the starting block. He presented numerous ideas—some of which were very interesting—but nothing happened. It can be like that with Greens. They recognize a good idea as quickly as anyone else. But, for example, while their Red colleagues sprint off with the baton, a Green just sits and waits. Often they're waiting for the right feeling to convince them of an idea's merit and if that doesn't happen, well . . . they wouldn't do anything anyway, so they get what they want. Why not just wait and see if the urge to act goes away?

This particular boss called in his employees and asked them how they viewed the business. He was worried about the evident lack of discernible commitment. A couple of the men, who were lower middle age, said straight-out that they couldn't think of anything that was worth getting involved in. The boss became extremely frustrated. He tried everything but got virtually no reaction.

This can also happen in a marriage. There are stereotypes for everything. Like that some women might be drawn to the strong, silent type, for example. Nothing wrong with that. But after they're married and she realizes that this is all that he is—strong and silent—she may not be as happy. And when she makes plans and he says he doesn't care, she gets frustrated. And so she makes even bigger plans. And he clutches the armrests on his favorite recliner even harder.

This is the paradox. The bigger the plans, the less likely it is that a Green will commit. All he wants is peace and quiet.

Here's an example: I've been writing fiction for twenty years and really hoped to become a published author one day. Everyone in the family knew this. Not that I made a huge deal out of it, but I didn't hide my ambitions, either. One Green close to me understood how important it was for me to succeed. I have repeatedly spoken about my dream, explaining how it would make me feel if I succeeded as an author of fiction. Yet this Green never asked how my writing was going. Maybe a comment every five years that I shouldn't take things so seriously or I will only be disappointed. And when I said things like: "This year it will happen. Now is the time, damn it. I've got to work harder to succeed!" the response was: "Wow. That's a lot of work." Lots of work is a Green's greatest enemy, just because that's exactly what it is—work. They live in a mind-set that everything should be easy.

This form of indifference and lack of commitment can kill the enthusiasm of even the most inspired person. I had to learn to rely on others to find the energy to struggle on with my writing. But a Green doesn't understand this. He doesn't want people to be too involved, because it's just bothersome. Instead, let's just sit here and do . . . nothing.

What's Thought in Secret Is Said in Secret

Greens are reluctant to take a position on sensitive issues. They have just as many views and opinions as anyone else, but they don't like shouting them from the rooftops. The reason is simple—it can cause a fuss.

The consequence of this tendency is a rather abstruse manner of expressing themselves. Instead of saying, "That's impossible," they may respond with something like, "It appears that there are a few challenges in delivering that." Sure, both statements mean the same thing: "We won't manage to do it in time." But by using a less direct means of expression, you take fewer risks. If you take a clear stance on something, then you have to stand up for it.

For a Green, it's better to be safe than sorry. By expressing himself ambiguously, he avoids taking responsibility for the matter in question. He doesn't have to risk his good name if he's uncertain. If he hasn't taken a position in support of something, he also hasn't taken any position against something. You hear how illogical this sounds, right? But if you're Green, you know exactly what I mean. A woman I met once said that she believed what everyone else believed.

But are Greens perceived as unclear just because they want to save a relationship? No, not at all. Greens just aren't as precise as the other colors. When a Red says that he absolutely hates listening to Eminem, a Green would say that he remembers better singers. When a Blue says that he has lost five pounds since last Tuesday morning at 10:03, a Green says that he's lost a few pounds lately.

This is because Greens are not as task oriented as Reds and Blues. Greens don't speak about facts in the same way. They would rather speak about relationships and feelings, which makes it more difficult to be precise. How do you measure a feeling? Saying, "I love you exactly twelve percent more than last month," is just not going to work.

"I Know I Should Change This Immediately, but I'll Just Think About It for a While."

Here we have the most difficult stumbling block. If you want to make changes in a group consisting of many Greens, good luck. If it's a major change, you should consider whether it's really worth the effort. If it's urgent, you can forget the whole thing. This is what happens in the mind of a Green:

- I know what I have but not what I'll get.
- It was better before.
- I've never done this before.
- The grass is not always greener on the other side.

Sound familiar? Sure, not all changes are for the better, but let's be reasonable! I'm not saying that it's always wrong to express these sentiments, but when changes are really necessary it can be very dangerous.

A classic cliché—a little worn now, I know—is to consider how often you change where you sit at the breakfast table. I used to ask this question in the groups I met. Many smiled and said that they sat where they usually sit because it just happened. Sure, I do the same thing sometimes. But if someone were to point out that I was stuck in a rigid habit (or bad habit) I would do something about it. A Green, however, doesn't correct himself.

When you look at a Green's reaction to the question, you'll understand that we're faced with a problem. I've seen adults become white in the face, wiping their foreheads at the mere thought of sitting on the other side of the table. I've even worked with a man, Sune, who had such a meticulous lunchtime routine that if he couldn't follow it precisely the rest of the day was shrouded in sheer darkness. Sune had a favorite lunch spot beneath a painting. He sat there every day at lunchtime, week in, week out, month out and year in. Always the same chair.

If he came into the dining room and saw that his spot was occupied, he would stop short. If he saw this quickly enough, he'd turn towards his backup location, not as good but still an acceptable spot, near a window. If he were forced to have his soup there, he would glare throughout the meal at whoever had nicked "his" spot. Of course, he never said anything. Instead, he just sulked the rest of the day. This is another thing Greens often do—turn frustration inwards and feel awful so that everyone notices it. If Sune's backup spot was also occupied, he would just go back into the kitchen, the rest of his day ruined.

Let me give you another example. My mother—departed but never forgotten; we'll never stop loving you, our darling mother—who was nothing if not Green, was always willing to help and took care of her grandchildren whenever needed, especially when they were little. I remember one time when my wife and I were invited to dinner on a Friday night. I had asked my mother to watch the kids weeks in advance because I knew that she needed time to mentally prepare herself for it.

On the day the dinner was to take place, the hostess called: Her husband was sick, and the whole thing was postponed. When I phoned my mum, I explained to her what had happened. We would be staying home that night. She went completely silent. I said that I still wanted her to come over because the children were excited to see their grandma.

Mum was very hesitant. "What will happen now?" she asked.

I said that it would be just like we had planned originally. Because her bag was packed and the guest room was ready, it would be a perfect opportunity to spend a little time together. She hesitated. "It will be completely different now: You're at home." She was flustered by the change, and she needed time to think. She promised to phone back.

What was really Mum's problem? Our change of plans necessitated no change for her at all. She was still going to stay overnight between Friday and Saturday. She could still see her grandchildren. She would, however, avoid having any responsibility for them. I tried to convince her that we could take care of her for once, instead of her taking care of us.

This was a completely new situation for her. We were still there in the house. And that was the problem. My wife and I would be there. Maybe Mum had her heart set on a watching a particular show on television. Maybe she had thought about preparing a special meal for the children. Maybe, I don't know. She never said anything about it, so we can't know for sure. But the change was serious enough to warrant extra thinking time for her.

(She came in the end. A nice little side story, quite possibly related to her generation: I fetched her at half past four. She asked why I came so late. I replied that I had promised to be there at five o'clock and that I was actually half an hour early. Her response? She'd been ready since four o'clock.)

"I've Never Been So Upset, but for God's Sake, Don't Say Anything to Anyone."

This is the second major dilemma with Green behavior. They despise a squabble. This aversion to conflict also causes many other challenges, such as stubbornness, ambiguity, and resistance to change. Because Greens are pronounced relational people, nothing is more important to them than keeping a relationship together. The problem is that their method doesn't work.

You can look at conflicts in two ways. The first way is called the harmony outlook, or striving for harmony. Everything depends on being on good terms with others. Reaching an agreement is an end in itself. This means that those who cause conflict are problematic troublemakers. Conflicts are indicative of poor leadership, poor communication, and discord. And so we smother conflict and pretend that it doesn't exist. Because who wants to be acquainted with a trouble-maker?

I once met a coach who used an interesting metaphor for this kind of behavior. She said it was like sitting at the dinner table with a rotting pile of trash in the middle. You know, with mold and flies and everything. Everyone sees that the trash is there, but no one says anything. You brush away the flies and pass the food across the liquefying banana peels without thinking anything about it. Maybe by the end someone wonders if there even really is a pile of trash on the table at all. Finally, one of the dinner table guests says, "We have to do something about this!" That person becomes an agitator, because we now have to deal with this nasty mess of garbage. Couldn't she have just kept quiet?

Nowadays we know better. The aspiration of having everyone in agreement about everything all the time is an impossible utopia, not even worth trying to achieve. Someone will lift the lid off all that discord that was so effectively and hermetically sealed for such a long period of time—and what happens then? It stinks from a long way off. In the end the harmony outlook inevitably leads to conflict.

The second way, and the opposite to the first, is called the conflict outlook. It basically means that we accept that conflicts exist—that it's natural. No group exists where everyone is always in agreement about everything.

The whole point of the conflict outlook is to deal with every little dissentient issue as soon as it shows its head. Reds, and also some Yellows, do this naturally. When they see something that doesn't work, they say that it doesn't work. This means that problems can be resolved at an early stage. But you have to deal with the issue before it begins to stink.

The conflict approach usually creates harmony.

But a Green will just turn a deaf ear. He'll do everything in his power to maintain that magical feeling that everyone is in agreement.

It's nicer when everyone agrees, isn't it? Wouldn't the world be so much better if there were no conflicts?

Consider a situation all of us have experienced at some point. We're in a meeting at work. There are maybe ten people present in the room. Add or subtract from this so that you recognize the situation. Someone—the boss or anyone at all—has just completed his presentation and now asks what everyone is thinking. Full of expectation, he looks around, waiting for feedback.

If there are any Reds or Yellows in the room, they will speak about their views on the proposal they've just seen. The Reds will love it or loathe it. The Yellows will speak about their own reflections on the proposal. One or two Blues might have a few questions.

What do the Greens do? Absolutely nothing. They just lean back in their chairs and let themselves absorb the proposal. They say nothing at all unless asked a direct question. They look anxiously around, hoping that someone will say that this proposal is, in fact, an incomprehensible mess. The group is too large for them to trot out any dissenting opinions. To say something truly dramatic or negative would mean that everyone's eyes will be on you, and that's not going to happen. If they say what they are really thinking, a heated debate will erupt, and since a Green doesn't want to take part in heated debates— he doesn't even want to be in the same room as one—he simply keeps silent.

How will the speaker respond? He'll assume that everyone is in agreement, right? What he doesn't know is that half the people in the room think it was the stupidest thing they have ever heard. When the truth creeps out—it has to, sooner or later—guess what happens then? Exactly—conflict.

You can be certain that while you are standing at the coffee machine and maybe even while visiting the restroom the truth will come out. When Greens need to relieve the pressure of not speaking out, they talk behind your back. In small groups of two or three people, they will gladly vent their displeasure. And they're good at it. As long as they think they can escape your gaze, they'll backbite you in ways you would never expect from a Green.

How Blue People Are Perceived

Even perfectionist Blue individuals receive criticism. It can be about how they are perceived as evasive, defensive, perfectionist, reserved, fastidious, meticulous, hesitant, conservative, lacking independence, questioning, suspicious, tedious, aloof, and coldhearted. Ooph! The list of shortcomings found in these bastions of bureaucracy often tends to be quite long.

But mainly, Blues find it difficult to begin anything new because they want to prepare very thoroughly. Everything involves risks, and Blues can be almost obsessed with details. Never place too many Blues in the same group. They'll plan into the next century without ever putting a shovel to the ground.

Furthermore, many Blues are perceived as highly critical and almost suspicious. They miss nothing, and they have a tendency to deliver their observations in an insensitive fashion. They create quality work, but their hairsplitting, critical approach to almost everything lowers the morale of those around them to dangerously low levels. These are people who consider themselves to be realists. When they—in everyone else's eyes—are, in fact, pessimists.

"Ninety-five Percent Right Is Actually 100 Percent Wrong."

Let's be honest from the start. All this keeping track of facts and focusing on details can go too far. There are limits to when it's reasonable to keep researching. Do you remember the CEO who wanted to buy leadership training? He never left the starting block.

Blues want to have all the information on everything, and this can lead to problems with those around them. People who would be satisfied with good enough simply can't cope with hearing all those questions and all this relentless poking into details. A Blue believes that good enough is never really good enough.

I enjoy working around the house—changing the decor, hanging wallpaper every now and then. A few years ago, we remodeled our kitchen, and even though I got tremendous help from my family, I did quite a lot myself. I worked and toiled and was quite happy when it was finished. For a DIYer, I thought I managed it quite well.

Hans, a good friend of mine, came by. We've known each other for many years, and he's very much on the ball. He knew that I'd worked very hard and that I felt quite pleased with myself. When he came into my kitchen, he looked around and said quietly, "New kitchen? Looks good. That cupboard door is crooked."

Okay, so maybe it wasn't nice to hear that. But for Hans, it was the highest form of logic. He observed a mistake and his sense of perfection meant that he couldn't ignore it. Besides, he is not a typical relational person, so he couldn't help saying things as they were. He wasn't directly criticizing me, only something I had done. Namely, not fitting the cupboard door straight.

Fastidiousness can be expressed in various ways: It can be a person who can't cope with papers that aren't perfectly aligned on a desk, who rewrites an email about fifteen times to get it truly perfect, or who works for hours on a simple Excel spreadsheet or PowerPoint presentation, just giving it the finishing touches.

They Never Finish Anything. There's Always More to Do.

Once, I was holding a communication training program for a group of people, all of who were working in the same room. The group consisted of about twenty people. The first afternoon, I handed out the results of the behavior analysis that each of them had taken earlier. Everyone read about themselves with increasing fascination, and most of them seemed very satisfied.

Except for one lady. She was extremely upset by her analysis. It was, in fact, completely incorrect. After confirming with her that it was okay to discuss it in front of the whole group, I asked what it was she was displeased with.

"There's so much that's incorrect," she told us. For example, the analysis revealed that she could be a perfectionist. She wasn't like that at all. I noticed the tiny smiles appearing on people's faces. Apparently, her colleagues knew something she didn't.

I asked her why she thought that the analysis maintained she was a perfectionist. She had no idea. The whole thing was a complete mystery. It was a totally useless tool.

Realizing that the woman was Blue, I was careful not to argue too much. She wouldn't take me at my word. I was just some random consultant who had been working with this tool for a measly twenty years. What did I know?

Instead, I asked her to give an example showing that she was not a perfectionist. No problem, she had plenty. For example, she had three children, each of who had three best pals. When she came home in the evenings, there were so many shoes piled up inside the front door that she had to do the high jump to get in. She began by shaking the dirt off the doormat and putting the shoes in order. She confided in me that she used to put size 10 at the back, as those guys went home last, so it seemed most logical. She placed the smaller sizes closest to the door in neat rows.

Then she went into the kitchen. What did she see there? Crumbs everywhere. All of these youngsters had been eating sandwiches, and the kitchen looked like a war zone. It took her twenty minutes to sanitize everything, put everything back in place, sweep, wipe the tables and worktops. Only then could she take off her coat and relax a little.

Her colleagues were in stitches. The woman looked around, not understanding what the excitement was all about. That any of this could even be remotely obsessive was beyond her. Her house was so untidy, that was her point.

The funny thing about this story is that a few years later I met the same woman but in a totally different context. She gave me a big hug and said that the analysis of her behavior was 100 percent correct. Stunned, I wondered how she arrived at that conclusion.

It turned out that she had kept the behavior profile in her purse for a while; the analysis had a list of behaviors and qualities, and every time she found herself doing one she ticked it off on the sheet. In the end, she had ticked all of them off. She liked the profile. An amazing tool, on the whole.

"I Don't Really Know You, So Keep Your Distance."

You've done it. I've done it. We've all done it. Gone up to a person who seems to be a decent fellow and started talking about this and that thinking you're going to have a nice chat. After a while, you realize that you're the one doing all the talking. If you have Yellow traits in your behavior, you may notice that there are strange pauses in the dialogue. If there really is a dialogue. You may notice that the other person fidgets a bit, signaling that he doesn't want to be part of this conversation.

"What's going on? We're just talking about the game yesterday, or about what the family did last summer, or where you intend to go on vacation. Do we have a problem, or what?"

Yes, in fact we do, because this person doesn't willingly speak with strangers. "Wait a minute," you may say. "We've been working together for three months, and by now it should be perfectly okay to ask what his dog's name is." But this guy requires a lot of personal space, both physically and psychologically. He needs to know a person extremely well before opening up. Not like a Red, who lets out with whatever he feels; not like a Yellow, who reveals his darkest secrets because he assumes that everyone is interested; or like a Green, who can be personal, but only in small groups and in a controlled environment.

A Blue doesn't need small talk. He can easily give the impression that he doesn't care about other people, because he doesn't cultivate any relationships. Sure, he cares, but his needs are on a different level than everyone else's. He likes being in his own company and with immediate family.

The consequence is clear for those around him: They find him cold-hearted and distant. That personal bubble is obvious, and it can be very chilly, particularly for Yellows and Greens. And so they call their Blue friend a bore. Blues can easily make us feel ill at ease. "Why is he so cold and dismissive? Doesn't he care about me at all?"

"Better Safe Than Sorry. Think About it—Preferably Three Times."

A good family friend couldn't leave her house without first checking to see if her keys were really in her handbag, even though placing them there was the last thing she had done before going to the front door.

Back in the 1980s, when I worked as a teller in the bank, I served people who had waited thirty minutes in line for just one single reason: to check that the balance printed on the ATM receipt really was correct. Much anticipation. The same computer. The same balance. But you never know. Best to check. And double-check. If a triple check had been possible, they would have done it.

Where does this need for control come from? Why can't Blues trust what other people say or just accept the information they hear? Answer: They can, of course. But if they also check themselves, then all the risks will be eliminated, right? But the fact remains that they don't trust others. Everything has to be confirmed. And recorded, and documented properly.

Remember, we're talking here about behavior as perceived by

others. A Blue checks everything one extra time because it's possible to check everything one extra time. When everything has been confirmed, then you just have to make a decision.

I have a good friend who uses Excel diligently. But not like the rest of us. This guy has a special method. He writes a formula and inserts all the data. Before he sends any important files to his senior managers, he does a control check of everything using a calculator.

Why does he do that?! If you were to explain this to a Red, he would declare that guy an absolute idiot. Explain it to a Yellow and he would laugh himself to death. Any Blue will understand the whole thing immediately. There is a theoretical possibility that there could be errors in Excel. Even though he has typed the formula himself, something may still go wrong. Better to be on the safe side.

How do others perceive this? Read on!

"The Only Thing I Can Trust Is Myself and My Own Eyes."

The guy who questions Excel has, of course, a problem explaining himself. Many people around him have their views about his method of always having to double-check and triple-check everything he does himself and everything everyone else does. They get furious when he, through his actions, clearly shows that he doesn't trust them.

The other tiny little problem is that everything takes a terribly long time. This can be managed by working more hours. What's more problematic is the way relationships can suffer because of this habit. How demoralizing is it when you go up to someone to tell him about a possible breakthrough and the first thing the person does is isolate all the different components and call into question every single point?

Of course, if everyone looks long enough they will find mistakes.

Nor is it even sufficient to be right. You have to prove yourself to a Blue. If he considers you an authority in a particular field, he'll be better at listening to you. The road, however, can be tricky.

I've held many training courses and lectures on this subject, and if there are people who ask complicated questions they're usually engineers, technical sales staff, or financial controllers. Maybe a handful of tax lawyers. Oftentimes their color is Blue, and they're not impressed with me. Just because I have made my living doing this for twenty years doesn't mean I know what I'm talking about. (Remember the woman who was accused of being a perfectionist.)

The only thing you can do is accept that among these people, the standard of proof will be much higher. Facts always remain, as we know: If I have prepared well enough I can prove that what I am saying is true. In time, they will trust me.

9

Learning New Things

How to Use What You've Learned

Learning something new isn't always the easiest of tasks. It may seem simple, but it's not easy. There's always so much to do, so much to read, and so much to learn. Where do you start? This is almost always determined by your personal interests. Naturally, it's easier to devote more time to what you're curious about and what you're interested in. Nothing strange there.

For me, it was hearing Sture's assessment of people—his thesis on all the idiots at the start of this book—that became the impetus for me to learn about people and how we relate to one another. But it's taken me many years to acquire this knowledge. I've read books, attended training, and been certified many times in different subjects. Furthermore, I've led thousands of courses on the subject. So now, as a middle-aged man, I believe I have a decent grasp on how people function. But, in all probability, I've only scratched the surface.

If We Had Endless Time,
There'd Be No Problem

All of this learning has taken time. Maybe I don't have the natural instinct that many others have. I don't really know. But I do know a bit about teaching methods and how we learn new things. And for me, it's difficult to think of any subject more important than people. No matter what job you have, where life may take you—you are going to meet other people.

For example, you can be:

- an employee with work colleagues
- a seller with customers
- a project manager who leads people with different expertise than your own
- a managing director with employees
- a middle manager with people both above and below you in the organization
- a self-employed entrepreneur finding your own sales and orders
- a parent with teenagers in the household
- a spouse
- a coach for the football team
- a chairperson of the local home and school associations

There's no limitation to how this knowledge can be applied. Understanding people will always remain a crucial factor in achieving your goals in life as smoothly as possible, no matter what these goals are.

Take a look at the diagram on the next page. This isn't a new model, but it says a lot about how theoretical knowledge is transformed into real competence. Reading a book is one thing—I'm glad that you are reading this one. It's a great way to kick off your own learning, but it's only the first step in learning something.

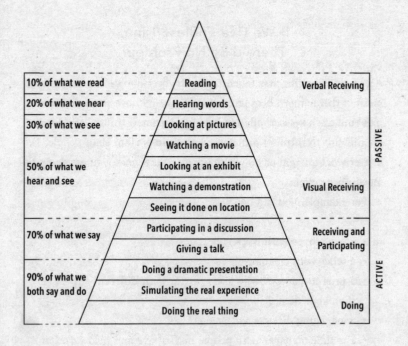

A New Approach

My mission is clear—I want more people to understand this method of classifying behavior. So much conflict could be avoided if we just understood why the people around us behave the way they do. I have nothing against conflict; it usually doesn't bother me, because I know how to handle it. But when people tear down and destroy more than they build up, I believe that we should be able to find other ways forward. Life consists of so much more than learning from your mistakes. Some mistakes you can avoid altogether.

A Language like Any Other Language

The "language" this book discusses—DISA-language IPD (the Institute for Personal Development) which is the official name—works like any other language when it comes to learning. If you've ever studied

Spanish or German in school, then you know what I'm talking about. To study for your exams is one thing. To be able to really speak fluently is a different matter. It's not enough to refresh your knowledge once a year just before a trip to Spain. If you really want to be able to speak Spanish (more than just ordering food at a restaurant) whenever you run into a Spanish speaker, you need to practice. It's a perishable commodity. There are no shortcuts.

Of course, after reading this book you can go out into the world and happily experiment with the people you meet. I advise you to do so. In the beginning, the challenge will be that you're going to guess incorrectly about people's personalities and that may result in a certain degree of embarrassment. But as you become more "fluent" in the language of behavior, it will transform how you interact with the people around you.

10

Body Language: Why How You Move Matters

How Do You Really Look?

Introduction

Different colors exhibit different types of body language. In addition to all things you say and do, you project a certain type of body language to the people around you. People pick up on this body language and use it to interpret your mood. So let's take a closer look at how we move.

"Body language" refers to all forms of nonverbal communication, conscious as well as unconscious. Differences in body language vary both between individuals and between different groups of people. Our body language also functions as a social and cultural marker, even if there are common biological foundations.

The modern English language contains about one hundred and seventy thousand words, of which five thousand are used regularly. In comparison, according to certain scholars, body language contains almost seven hundred thousand signals. Yes, we can debate the exact numbers, but that's not the point. Just understand that there are an immense number of signals, more than we may be aware of.

I'm not going to examine all these signals, but it's still interesting to see what the differences are between different behavior profiles. Just remember, our state of mind, situation, and whether we feel safe or unsafe can have a crucial influence on our body language.

Posture

If on the one hand, you have a relaxed, natural but not slack posture, other people often get the impression that you are self-confidence. If on the other hand, you have a shrunken posture, it can be interpreted as resignation and disappointment. If you have an erect, somewhat wooden posture, people can believe that this is a signal of dominance; in other words, you demand respect from those around you. However, it could also be an indication that you were trained at a military academy.

Gaze

We use our eyes for many different things. Shifty eyes generally suggest that the person in question would rather be somewhere else. Other people meet your gaze steadily, without even blinking. This creates a totally different impression. It's said that liars can't look you in the eye and they often shift their gaze to the side. But since this is commonly known even among liars, the worst of them have learned to stare you straight in the eyes when they are lying. So nothing is that obvious. (Someone who is repeatedly touching his neck is more often an indicator of a liar.) When something is awful or unpleasant, many lift their hands up to their faces. And when you need to think, you often close your eyes for a while.

Head and Face

When speaking, we usually either nod or shake our heads, depending on whether we agree or not. When we listen extra carefully to a discussion, we can lean our heads to one side. Hanging your head or wrinkling your forehead can signal sadness or depression. When we're amazed at something, we often raise our eyebrows, while we turn up our noses at things we aren't fond of. In your face alone forty-three different muscles are concealed, and these can be combined in countless ways.

Hands

Yes, this is a true classic. When greeting a person, how hard do you really have to shake his hand? A simple handshake can reveal a lot about a person. Limp and feeble handshakes often indicate a submissive behavior, so if you have such a handshake it might be a good idea to press a little harder. If a handshake is firm it probably suggests that a person is determined. Anyone who squeezes way too hard belongs more than likely to the former category but would prefer to belong to the latter. Clenched fists rarely mean good news, usually indicating aggressiveness. Certain nervous people pick at their clothes, removing hairs or threads. This often indicates they would rather focus their attention on other things. Holding your hands clasped behind your back often expresses power and security.

Remember what I just said about lies? A more effective way to spot a liar is to notice if he puts the palm of his hand on his chest—preferably his right hand over his heart—and sighs indignantly when he's been accused of lying. "Would I lie? How can you say that about me?" This gesture is intended to strengthen his honest intentions, but it immediately puts those around on their guard, because it is so unnecessary and excessive. There's definitely something fishy going on there.

Territory

It's very important that all people have their own personal space, as everyone needs an area that is his own. Among other things, this territory can be the distance you maintain from people when you're speaking to them. The personal zone is generally a few feet and the social zone is three to ten feet. When we speak about the personal zone we mean the space when two people who know each other are communicating. "The social zone" refers to the space between strangers who are communicating. But this is very much dependent on the culture of the speakers. In the Nordic European region, for example, the personal zone is definitely larger than what someone from the Mediterranean would have.

So What Do We Do About All This?

How do the various forms of behavior differ from one another? It's obvious that some "well-known" facts about body language don't apply to every single person. Someone who is busily picking lint off his sleeve might be bored or he might just be nervous. Another example is how people deal with uncertainty. A Green who is unsure leans backwards. A Red who is unsure leans forward, as his way of dealing with this uncertainty is to try to dominate the conversation. On the following pages, I've listed further examples of the differences. Try observing people in real life to see if you can find any of the following forms of behavior. But remember, body language is very individual. Sure, there are the general expressions that apply throughout the entire world and among all people—a contemptuous stare, for example, looks similar in every country—but there are so many differences that you'll have to study your fellow mortals to sharpen your ability. The following short sections are intended to serve as a simple guide.

Red Body Language

Some basics to keep in mind about Reds. They:

- keep their distance from others
- have powerful handshakes
- lean forward aggressively
- use direct eye contact
- use controlling gestures.

As I mentioned previously, Reds often have a clear and distinctive body language. You can usually recognize a Red from a distance.

When you walk through large crowds, you'll see people swarming around, standing still, conversing with others, or just checking to see what all the fuss is about. Let's say that you're looking at a town square teeming with people. If you look really closely, you will see a person who is crossing the square at a brisk pace completely disregarding the people standing in his way. With his gaze fixed on a point a bit in front of him, the Red speeds up and crosses the square without any problem. He does not give way but makes others move aside. His steps are decisive and powerful. He expects the rest of us to get out of his way.

The first time you meet a Red, he usually maintains a certain distance. His handshake won't be hearty, but it will be powerful. Expect that the Red—man or woman—will grip a little bit harder to show who is in charge. (Some people consider this alpha male behavior, but it also occurs in women. A Red has a need to demonstrate that he is someone to be reckoned with.)

Forget overexuberant smiles. His face can be downright grim, especially if you're attending a business meeting. But even in social settings, Reds maintain some reserve. A Red won't give you a big bear hug (as long as he is sober; under the influence of alcohol, anything can happen).

When things start getting tense—which usually happens rather quickly when Reds are involved—this guy will lean across the table and argue his case quite forcefully. Eye contact will be very direct, his gaze fixed on you. When it comes to the language of power, Reds have their finger on the trigger right from the start. Be prepared for that.

Also, be prepared for a relatively limited use of gestures, but those gestures that do surface can be controlling and aggressive. Reds point at people very readily. The notion that it is rude to point at people isn't something that particularly worries him. It's also common that Reds point at you by stretching out their hand towards you with the palm facing down. If you want to give this a try, ask someone to point at you that way, and then think about how it feels.

You can also clearly see that Reds—of course they are not alone in this—are more than willing to interrupt you. They draw their breath continuously, hoping to find gaps in the conversation. If they have to wait too long to speak, they'll throw themselves into the conversation with a loud voice and simply take over.

VOICE

What about a Red's tone of voice? It's often strong. We hear these people clearly because they think nothing of raising their voices to make themselves heard—as much as it takes. Of course, even Reds can be nervous and worried about things, but usually you won't hear this. Their voices won't tremble that much.

This is one of the secrets Reds have. No matter what's happening behind the façade, Reds will sound convincing. No stammer, no hesitation. Finger on the trigger. If we don't listen, they will repeat it one more time, but louder. In the end, they always get through.

SPEED IN SPEECH AND DEED

As I mentioned earlier, Reds are always in a hurry. Quick equals good. Normally, this even applies to speech and actions. Everything happens at a furious pace. Because speed is the factor many Reds measure success by, it will be all go. And a couple of sharp changes when the course needs adjusting.

Yellow Body Language

Some simple basics to keep in mind about Yellows. They:

- are tactile
- are relaxed and jocular
- show friendly eye contact
- use expressive gestures
- often come close.

A Yellow's body language is often very open and inviting. Smiles appear constantly, even when there's not much to smile about. They joke around a lot and can be very relaxed. When visiting a neighbor he doesn't know that well, a Yellow may just stretch out on the sofa. But this is typical for Yellows. When a Yellow feels secure in any given situation, you can see it. He's like an open book.

The similarity with Red behavior lies primarily in the tempo. Yellows move quickly and quite distinctively. They often radiate a strong self-confidence.

Personal space is a relative thing for Yellows. While some colors don't like having people sit too close to them, Yellows will willingly move up very close. Yellows can spontaneously start hugging everyone around them. Man or woman, it doesn't really matter. It depends on what the feeling and the mood are that day.

It's not uncommon for others to recoil when this happens, which Yellows find very trying. But it's not just that Yellows like hugging. It can also be a simple form of physical contact. A hand placed on an arm, a pat on the leg—with no ulterior motive. The Yellow just wants to reinforce what he's said. What a Yellow perceives as something natural and spontaneous others can perceive as an invitation. And of course, it can end badly.

In general, with Yellows there will be jokes all round and countless smiles. Eye contact is no problem; it's intense, cheerful, and friendly.

VOICE

A Yellow's tone of voice denotes a strong commitment from start to finish. You hear it from afar: Laughter, fun, intensity. Enthusiasm. Joy. Energy.

Generally speaking, Yellows show empathy very clearly. They're with you either 100 percent or not at all. And this can be heard in their voice. It goes up and down; it changes tempo, vigor, and intensity. Yellows often have a powerful melody in their way of speaking.

No matter what emotion has seized the Yellow at the moment, it will be noticeable in his voice.

SPEED IN SPEECH AND DEED

Tempo. Not quite the same rate of action as Reds, but a decidedly fast pace. Have you met anyone who, when in a hurry to say something, kind of stumbles over his words? Only half of them really come out as they should. You can surmise what is being said, but sometimes it's incomprehensible. These are Yellows whose mouths simply can't keep up with everything they have to say.

Green Body Language

Some simple basics to keep in mind about Greens. They:

- are relaxed and come close
- act methodically
- tend to lean backwards
- use very friendly eye contact
- prefer small-scale gestures.

Greens are often—but not always—sluggish in body movement. When they're completely harmonious, they have a relaxed body language that exudes calm and confidence. No impetuous movements, no sudden tossing of their heads or hands. Nice and easy.

Their gestures are often less flamboyant and well suited for smaller groups. Greens don't feel at ease in larger groups, so they become more closed and will appear reserved. Greens often have body language that gives them away. They try to hide their true feelings but don't always succeed. If they're out of balance or feel uncomfortable, it will be visible.

When sitting around a table, you can expect that Greens will tend to lean backwards. This is something of a paradox, as they don't really have a problem getting close to people. Just like Yellows, they like to touch others. It's fine as long as they know the person they are touching. Beware, however, of touching a Green who hasn't given a clear sign that he knows you well enough. It's easy to cross the line. They can be protective of their personal space.

You often notice when a Red walks across a room. Since Greens are the complete opposite of Reds in many things, I can say that Greens make discretion a point of honor. It's not uncommon that they try to make themselves invisible.

The reason? They don't want to be the center of attention.

Greens almost always have friendly faces. If not, then they're quite neutral. Don't expect any exaggerated smiles or overexuberant greetings. A little expectant, that's it. But the difference will be huge if a Green knows you. If he thinks that you are good friends, he can be very intimate and friendly. If he feels that you have just met each other, well then, you just have to wait.

Let Greens come to you. Do not force yourself on them. In time, when they trust you, they'll relax and become more natural.

VOICE

A Green's voice will never be strong; it's not likely that he will drown out the group. You'll have to make a little bit more effort. Even when Greens speak in front of a larger group (they may do this, if they don't have any choice), they'll speak as if there were only three of you sitting around the table. Sometimes it may appear that Greens don't see the other hundred people in the room. The volume is generally low, and it can be difficult to hear what they say.

But their voice will always be soft and radiate warmth. The pace will be slower and the variation not at all like when a Yellow speaks.

SPEED IN SPEECH AND DEED

Generally, Greens have a slower pace than Reds and Yellows but not quite as slow as Blues. Speed has no value in itself. If a heightened tempo risks destroying the cooperation in the group, Greens will reduce the speed. It doesn't matter what the deadline is. The most important thing is always going to be how people feel.

Blue Body Language

Some simple basics to keep in mind about Blues. They:

- prefer to keep others at a distance
- either stand or sit

- often have closed body language
- use direct eye contact
- speak without gestures.

The easiest way to describe a Blue's body language is to say that he has none. Okay, maybe that is a bit simplistic. What I mean is that there's not that much to interpret in a Blue. Neither his face nor his body gives much away. When I speak about body language to sales-people, they usually remark that some people are impossible to inter-pret. When I ask if these are people who sit almost perfectly still without moving even a muscle in their faces, they usually nod and think this is remarkable.

They're probably talking about Blues. A person who doesn't exhibit much movement or even temperament reveals nothing. In this case, it's the lack of distinctive body language that tells us what we need to know.

Many Blues can make very dramatic statements with an expression-less face. I once heard a blue manager say that the department was to close and that we had to agree on a decommissioning plan for three hundred employees. Not a muscle in his face moved unnecessarily.

This is what gives people the idea that Blues lack feelings, but this is, naturally, not true. Let me remind you again that a Blue is an intro-vert, which is to say, most of his emotions simply operate beneath the surface.

It also works the other way. Once, many years ago, I saw a lady win a half a million dollars on television. Behind the camera her hus-band was heard screaming for joy, while the lady herself sat very still with a cool smile. The host smiled and waved his arms around, and for a while you had to wonder who had actually won. But the lady herself said nothing more than "Thank you, this was nice." She hardly moved at all. I don't think it was because she was already a millionaire; it was because she was Blue. This is simply the way it works. Beneath the surface, I assume that she was delighted with her winnings, but she didn't show it outwardly. One day I will call the channel and ask if they still have the recording, because it's such a vivid illustration.

When you see Blues speaking in front of larger groups, this tendency becomes very evident. Just like Greens, they have no need to be the center of attention. The difference, however, is that while a Green would like to sink through the floor, a Blue will remain standing. He'll try to whip up the masses while standing completely motionless with a fixed face.

Another clue is that Blues require a relatively large amount of personal space around them. They often feel more comfortable by keeping others at a distance. Naturally, it depends on how well they know each other, but this zone is significantly larger than it is for Yellows, for instance.

If others come too close, Blues' body language becomes closed. Both arms and legs will be crossed, indicating that they're keeping their distance.

As I mentioned earlier, Blues move less than others. When they stand, they stand still. There's not that much swaying and walking. They can very easily stand in the same spot for a whole hour while giving a lecture. When they sit down, they remain seated more or less in the same position all the time.

Consequently, they won't use too many gestures. Imagine a Yellow: a really outgoing and dynamic figure—and now think the opposite. Take away all movements that aren't needed (most of them, according to Blues) and you begin to get the picture. Stone-faced, as someone once described it.

However, Blues normally look others straight in the eyes. They have no problem with eye contact, even if it makes others uncomfortable.

VOICE

Though not exactly weak, a Blue's voice is restrained and subdued. They don't make much of a fuss about themselves. Their impression tends to be controlled. It's common for them to sound very pensive, as if weighing every word before it's allowed to see the light of day.

Generally, there's little or no variation in a Blue's voice. He sounds more or less the same all the time—whether he's reading the *TV Guide* or giving his acceptance speech to the nation after winning the presidential election. Without much rhythm or melody, he just continues to say what's on the script.

Musicians tend to have difficulty with this. They think everything a Blue says flows badly.

SPEED IN SPEECH AND DEED

Slow. At least if we compare it to others'. If we take a Red or even a Yellow, he'll speak at the speed of sound. A Blue has a completely different pace. It will take as long as it takes. Speed is of no interest.

11

A Real-Life Example: The Company Party—How to Understand Everyone You Meet

Many years ago, I used to work in the banking sector. It was an interesting job in many ways, though it could be a little humdrum at times. However, I learned a lot by meeting many different types of people, and I have many stories of funny customer meetings from that period. The most interesting insights, however, I gained behind the scenes.

One of the more startling experiences was at a branch where I was working in the 1990s. A series of behavior stereotypes were working there. Some of them were obvious in their behavioral profiles. We had incredibly distinctive Blues and equally obvious Greens and Yellows. And, of course, a Red boss.

One spring we'd been working incredibly hard, many had been out sick, and we were under pressure from customers. People were tired, irritated, and touchy. We really needed some good news. The person who got fed up with all the hard work first was one of the Yellow advisors. One day, she came into the lunchroom and said that she'd had enough of all our grumpy faces. We needed something fun to do, and she knew exactly what.

It was time to find a goal, something to look forward to. A company party would save the day! Full of enthusiasm, she told us that she'd seen a very nice conference center nearby where all of us could go for a weekend to have a good rest. They had a stunning spa and gym, snazzy hotel rooms, and a trendy restaurant that was truly a la mode. In addition, she knew the owner through a friend of a friend and could probably get a bargain price on the whole package. She just wanted to know what we thought about the idea.

At first, we all stared at her, not knowing if the whole thing was for real, because we suspected that she probably didn't know the owner at all. With a broad smile, she continued to speak, talking about all the fun we could have: We could play games, organize some friendly competitions, enjoy bubble baths, and, of course, have a monster party in the evening.

A lively discussion began, and several of us thought the idea sounded great. The Red bank director looked around and saw that his employees liked the idea. Thankfully, he was keen on the idea. We were tired and worn out, and he wanted to show his appreciation for our commitment. He made the decision right there and then. After a five-minute discussion, he declared that there would be a party and he promised to foot the bill.

He looked at the Yellow woman who had suggested the party and asked if she was prepared to organize everything. Make the necessary calls and book everything. She immediately began to deliver a long harangue that was nothing more than one big smoke-screen to hide the fact that she thought she had done her bit by coming up with the idea. The Red boss silenced her with a wave of his hand. A few Green colleagues were sitting behind him on a corner of the sofa, the same corner where they always sat. The boss didn't even need to turn around to be able to call them by name. He asked each of them if they would help. They all agreed without really knowing what he'd asked. The Red boss nodded briefly and left the room. He was done. As he stood up, he forgot about the matter immediately.

Excitement burst forth, and everyone with Red and Yellow in their behavior profiles began exclaiming about the party, all talking at the same time. The Yellow advisor was extremely enthusiastic and continued to sell the idea, despite the fact that the decision had already been made. Her proposals for the type of party we should have became wilder and wilder. I remember that she started with a black-tie ball and had come all the way to a toga party before someone managed to silence her.

However, one person sat silently in the corner. Our Blue credit manager was very concerned. When everything calmed down a bit, he said with a loud voice, "But how are we supposed to get there?"

The only thing he had heard about the whole affair was that the conference center was twenty miles outside of town, and now the problems were stacking up. We were faced with a significant logistical challenge. Should we go by car? Or taxi? Or had the bank planned to charter a bus? How would this actually be done? Endless obstacles were lining up. He crossed his arms and clenched his teeth.

The Yellow woman erupted and tore into him right away. How could he be so negative? Here she was after coming with the best idea in the world and he immediately spoiled the whole thing with umpteen trying questions. Maybe he should come up with his own ideas for once? How did he think we should get there? He didn't have an answer; he just pointed out that there were lots of options. He couldn't make any decision or have an opinion. He only knew that the whole idea was poorly thought out.

The Greens saved the day by saying that they were willing to take their cars and pick everyone up. Five cars should be enough, and they promised to arrange everything. This announcement calmed the discussion down a little, and the Yellow woman could feel like a winner again. Her party had just been saved.

Everyone looked forward to the party, but the Yellow advisor never showed up; she had accidentally double-booked that day. There must have been a wedding on that same weekend. Or maybe a relative was turning fifty. As a matter of fact, it might have been both.

What Happens at a Company Party When No One Is Paying Attention

Once the party started, exciting things happened. We all know that alcohol affects people. We also know that different people are affected in different ways. Nothing strange so far. If we ignore for a moment that the amount of alcohol consumed is an important factor and assume that we're just talking about moderate drinking and that no one will drive their cars that night, we can see some interesting patterns.

We had several Yellows in our branch. The four sellers who dealt with private customers were very Yellow. They were jovial, positive entertainers right from the outset. They needed no alcohol before daring to "loosen up" and become approachable. In fact, you could easily get the impression that they always were a bit tipsy, because they had that frolicsome energy. They saw life as one long celebration that should always be funny and amusing.

But the interesting thing is that Yellows who drink can lose some of this. During the company party, I observed that three of the four Yellow salespeople became more and more silent as the evening went on. As the intake of certain beverages increased and the atmosphere became more intense, they withdrew. I remember one of the guys sat down on the steps outside with a wineglass in his hand. I asked him what was the matter. He was moody and philosophical. What was the point of it all? Why did he go the extra mile? No one ever really thanked him for it. Perhaps the best thing to do was to resign. My cheerful colleague had been transformed into a brooding pessimist.

Funnily enough, I found the Blue credit manager inside the party venue dancing on the table while telling dirty jokes. Never before nor since have I heard such dirty jokes. When I asked his colleagues what he had been drinking, they shrugged their shoulders and said that he always behaved like that when he got started. If I had met him for the first time that night, I would have thought that he was one of the Yellows at our workplace.

It was as if Yellows and the Blues had completely switched personalities. You could conclude that a really good party consists of sober Yellows and Blues who are slightly under the influence.

However, things became really interesting when I found our Red bank director, who normally was quite stern. He had a glass of whisky in his hand and was standing there speaking to the Green group of administrators. He explained, a little ambiguously I hasten to add, that he really wasn't a horrible person and that he liked them very much. When he lost his temper at the office, they shouldn't take it personally; he meant no offense, and they didn't need to be afraid of him.

The six Greens, two men and four women, who had been drinking as well, all spoke up and gave him a piece of their minds. They were irritated by his behavior and explained that he was the worst boss they'd ever had. Each of them had been working in the office for at least twenty years and when he was gone they would still be there, and what did he think about that? They backed him into a corner and gave him a proper dressing-down. The Red boss fled the field and was the first to leave the party.

Even the Reds and the Greens had changed behavior with each other in some strange way! I left the party with an extraordinary insight—alcohol changes people, but exactly how they change is even more interesting.

However, back in the office on Monday, everything was back to normal. The Yellows told their latest jokes, and the Blue guy did not say a word. The boss glowered at everyone, and the Greens just stared at the wall when he showed up. Order was restored.

Again, I cannot prove this, so you simply have to do your own research. Challenge your pals late on a Friday night and you'll understand exactly what I mean. Just take it easy with the alcohol.

12

Adaptation

How to Handle Idiots
(i.e., Everyone Who Isn't like You)

Now let's now take a look at how we can adapt to one another in order to work together. A man once said (admittedly with an ironic smile on his face, but still) that the test of intelligence is simple: "If you agree with me, then you're intelligent. However, if you don't agree with me, then you are clearly and undoubtedly an idiot."

I assume that you're intelligent enough to interpret this message correctly. But seriously—all of us have wondered why some people don't understand anything. As I said in the introduction, when I was young I was often struck by the fact that people who appear to be very intelligent could, at the same time, be such complete idiots. They didn't see what I saw. Some people delicately say that such individuals lack the right "intellectual elasticity," but that's only because they're too well bred to let the word "idiot" come out of their mouths.

People Are Obviously Different.
So What Do You Do About It?

How should we handle people who are different from us when they react and function in completely different ways? Can you take on various kinds of personalities in different situations? An interesting question. If it were possible to behave 100 percent like a chameleon—completely changing your behavior depending on whom you're with—would it be a good idea to try? It's natural for us to be who we are, to exhibit our own core behavior. But for a variety of reasons, we can feel the need to adapt to those around us. There's often a lot of talk about how we must be flexible and adaptable so that we can cope with a wide variety of situations and are able to respond to many different types of people. The term has even been given a name—EI (emotional intelligence) or EQ (emotional quotient). To cope with this constant need for adaptation, it's important that we're aware that adaptation demands effort and takes a lot of energy.

Our natural condition is to exhibit our core behavior. Our "unnatural" behavior is to continually adapt to others, and this requires ability, training, and energy. If we're uncertain as to what is "right" in a situation, if we're untrained or lack sufficient energy to cope with the role that we currently believe is the right one, we will be frightened, hesitant, and often stressed. As a result, we lose even more energy and our core behavior becomes increasingly visible—often to the great surprise of those around us, who are used to seeing us behave in a certain way.

In a Perfect World

In the best of worlds, everyone can be themselves and everything functions smoothly from the word go. Everyone agrees at all times and conflicts don't exist at all. This place is said to exist, and it's called Utopia. But it's not that simple. As I said at the beginning of this book, if you think that you can change everyone else, you'll be very disappointed. It would surprise me if you could change anyone at all.

No matter who you are—Red, Yellow, Green, or Blue, or a combination of multiple colors—you will always be in the minority. Most of the people you encounter will be different from you. No matter how well balanced you are, you can't be all the types at the same time. So you have to adapt to the people you meet. Good communication is often a matter of adapting to others.

But wait a minute, you might be thinking. That isn't true. I can be myself. In fact, I never adapt myself for anyone, anytime, and it's gone very well. It's taken me this far in life.

Absolutely.

Naturally, everyone can start with themselves. That's not a problem. But then, don't expect to get through to other people with the message you're trying to share. If you can live knowing that most of the people you meet won't buy what you say, well, then you don't have a problem.

You Already Do This, Even If You Don't Think You Do

You already adapt your behavior, even if you don't realize it. We all adapt to one another all the time. It's part of the social game, the visible and invisible communication that is constantly in progress. I'm just proposing a more reliable system. You don't have to gamble or guess. You can make the right adjustment from the beginning. But please note: usually. No system is perfect.

Some people I meet don't like the idea of deliberately adapting to others. They consider it dishonest and manipulative. But again, you can always abstain.

An Example from Real Life

I'm going to tell you a true story about a man I met during a training conference many years ago, a likeable and very popular private entrepreneur who achieved great success in his field. This man—let us call him Adam—was extremely Yellow, a real visionary with ambitious plans that were only occasionally put into effect.

Adam had never thought about or reflected on how he behaved as a person or how he was perceived by others. There had never been any reason to. Someone had persuaded him to come to this conference, and he didn't really know what he was getting himself into.

The topic that day was the same as this book; it was a full-day workshop where we worked on how to understand different behavior profiles. After the lunch break, I saw that something was troubling Adam. His face was serious, and his body language had become very closed. When I started talking again and explaining the various profiles, he sank deeper and deeper into his chair, and it was obvious to me that he was thinking about something else.

I asked what was troubling him.

There was an explosion. He exclaimed, "This is wrong! How could I categorize people like that? Put people into a theoretical grid system?" It turned out that he didn't like the idea of adapting to other types of people, but not because he thought that everyone had to adapt to him. No, what worried him was that he saw it as a way to manipulate others and he didn't like it. Didn't like it at all, in fact.

Everyone wondered what the real problem was. Adam believed that you couldn't categorize people this way. That using a lot of models was just wrong. He thought that it was highly dangerous not to go on pure feeling.

Someone in the group made it clear to him that he of all people should listen, since he was the one who attracted conflict. The debate was soon in full swing, and after thirty minutes I had to call a time-out.

I can understand Adam's concern, and I respect the fact that he raised the issue. What worried him was that it wouldn't work: If everyone adapted to one another, no one would be themselves any longer. In his way of thinking, that would be the greatest deception—not to be yourself.

There's something in what he said. At the same time, of course, you can always choose how much or little you modulate your behavior. The more you learn about other people, the easier it becomes for you to make decisions. Join in the game, or go your own way? The decision will always be yours.

Furthermore, Adam was also deeply resentful that I, as a specialist in the field, could describe him in quite some detail and give examples of how I thought he was wired. When he looked at the assessment tool that describes an individual, he went completely silent.

Ultimately, after we sat down and discussed the matter Adam came to understand the role and benefits of behavior assessment. But he taught me to be careful with how I use this knowledge.

How Often Do We Follow a System Without Knowing If It Works?

No system is perfect. There are always exceptions. This is just one piece in the jigsaw puzzle of human life. It's certainly a large and important piece, but it's far from the whole picture.

I've divided up the sections on adaptation into two parts for each color. The first part deals with what you need to do to interact meaningfully with another person—when you really want to get through to him and put him in a cheerful mood and make him feel that you understand him. The second part deals with how you get people to take your side. What each profile wants in a situation isn't necessarily the best thing to do to make progress.

You can do a great deal of good—if you choose to do so.

Adapting to Red Behavior

What a Red Expects of You

"DO WHAT I ASKED OF YOU, AS QUICKLY AS POSSIBLE–PREFERABLY, EVEN FASTER THAN THAT."

If you ask a Red, he'll agree that most people are too slow. They speak too slowly, they have trouble coming to the point, and they work ineffectively. In a Red's world, everything simply takes way too long.

Remember what I told you about impatience in Red behavior, about their constant pursuit of (fast) results. When other people turn things over in their minds from morning to night, it drives a Red crazy.

Thought and action are one. It has to be done quickly. If there's anything Reds dislike, it's endless discussion. It makes them flip out.

Conclusion: If you want to adapt to a Red's tempo—hurry up! Speed up! Speak and act more quickly. Look at the clock often, because that's what a Red does. If you can conclude a meeting in half the time—do it! If you have a Red with you in the car, he won't be upset if you're a little bit over the speed limit. (If you drive too slowly, he might insist on taking the steering wheel.)

"DO YOU WANT SOMETHING? SPEAK UP!"

As you now know, Reds are very much to the point, and they enjoy being with other people who also have the ability to tell them what they want—quickly. If you have a tendency to go around in circles before getting to the crux of the matter, you'll have difficulty getting through to a Red. He'll get tired if you waste your words without due cause. And he knows when he's dealing with a chatterbox.

It's very common for people to provide some background to a problem before describing the problem itself. And maybe even some more background to the solution of the problem.

Forget it. It won't work.

Conclusion: If you want to have a Red's full attention, cut the small talk. It's vital that you're clear and straightforward. Determine the most essential point of your message and start there. Let's say that you're going to present the latest financial statement. Say what's written on the last line of the slide first—that's what a Red is sitting there waiting for anyway. Then you can get into the details.

Don't use a single word unnecessarily. But make sure you've done your homework when it comes to the background. Questions may come up. If a Red senses that you're uncertain, you'll be grilled on the facts.

Written materials should be concise and, above all, well laid out. No endless dissertations written by someone who loves the sound of his own voice. A single line jotted down on the back of the napkin will do the job.

"I COULDN'T CARE LESS WHAT YOU DID ON VACATION."

Reds live in the present. Everything that happens is happening here and now. They have a unique ability to focus on what's on the current agenda. Thus, you need to stick to the topic when you speak to a Red. He has no problem with creativity or new ideas; this is always appreciated as long as it moves you forward. But when a Red feels that you've left the agenda altogether and are beginning to fiddle-faddle, then conflict isn't that far off.

The most effective method for a Red is to establish what the problem is and then just get to work. Simple, isn't it?

Conclusion: Stick to the topic! The easiest way is to prepare your case very precisely before going into a meeting with a Red. If, in the middle of an interesting discussion, another thought pops into your head, write it down and ask at the end of the meeting if it's okay to raise the issue. Otherwise, schedule a new meeting.

If someone with lots of Red in his behavior asks what time it is, answer the question with the exact time. Don't say that there's plenty of time. He'll decide that himself. And again—don't forget to keep up the pace. For a Red, "speed" will be synonymous with "efficiency."

Now we're talking business—never forget it. Being businesslike in business doesn't really sound like a novel idea, but think about it. If you're a seller, you've probably attended a number of training courses in sales where you learned that you have to build up a relationship with the customer. Get to know him. Win him over to your side.

This is good advice. Do it. Build relationships as much as you deem necessary. Just don't do it with Reds. For example, if you begin a meeting with a Red whom you've never met before, nothing could be worse than asking where he lives, where he spent his last vacation, or what he thought of the game last night. Nothing could be more irrelevant to him. He's not here to chat or make friends. He's there to do business. Deeply Red individuals become downright irritated and aggressive when they notice that someone is trying to be friends with them.

A Red is not here to be your pal. He's only here for one reason—to do business. He might throw you out—figuratively speaking—if he perceives your attempts to be friendly as ingratiation or fawning. This isn't something he would dream of doing himself, so neither should you.

And don't flatter a Red if you don't know him well. Just leave the compliments at home.

Conclusion: Paradoxically, Reds are the easiest to sell to. If you want to do good business, the only thing you need to do is step into a Red's office, present your suggestions, and then ask about a deal. Skip the football game yesterday. Never mind that you saw him in the supermarket last week. He didn't see you anyway. When a Red trusts you and has decided that you're a decent person who can be advantageous to him, well, then he may very well start discussing cars, boats, or the latest politics. Play ball with him. But then and only then. And don't be surprised if the meeting ends mid-sentence. When he's satisfied with his socializing, he concludes it instantly. It has nothing to do with you. He's just tired of conversation.

"YOU DON'T ACTUALLY KNOW? THEN WHY AM I WASTING MY TIME WITH YOU?"

It may sound like a contradiction, but a Red would also like you to be determined and direct. Although he often demands that he make all the important decisions himself, he strongly dislikes dealing with vacillating people. Dancing the hesitation waltz does not instill trust. Comments like "It's hard to say," "It depends," or "I don't really know what to say" just frustrate Reds.

If you have an opinion, out with it. Reds judge you on how driven you are. You should listen to them, of course, but you must have an opinion of your own. Otherwise, you're weak, and that's not a quality that will win you any points.

Keep in mind that we all like people in whom we can recognize ourselves. A Red won't meet other Reds every day, so when he actually does he's pleasantly surprised. "An equal! Wonderful!" I have met Reds who have rubbed their hands gleefully before starting a heated debate.

Conclusion: Deliver your opinion without blinking. In the end, you might have to concede, but never sell yourself short. A Red can rattle and rumble, stamp on the floor, raise his voice, and shake his fist. Many people back off in the face of this behavior. It's not pleasant to be shouted at, is it?

Well, the worst thing you can do is back away and let him walk all over you. If a Red is permitted to walk over you, you lose something very important in his eyes—respect. If he doesn't respect you, he'll eat you alive. And walk over you again and again and again until you become completely and totally marginalized. You won't be someone to be reckoned with in the future. A complete doormat.

The best thing you can do is place yourself in the center of the storm, telling him that he's wrong. When a Red discovers that you won't give in, he will turn in an instant. If you know what you are talking about, that is.

YOU CAN SLEEP WHEN YOU'RE DEAD

If you have a boss who is Red, he will work hard, maybe harder than anyone else you've ever met. He will have many irons in the fire at once, and he'll have complete control over everything that's happening.

A Red can live with the fact that everything won't be right the first time. But he will demand that you work hard. You should be diligent in everything; feel free to put in overtime if you can. I urge you not to become a workaholic—life has more to offer than work—but from the perceptive of a Red boss, this would be a first-class quality. He will hold you in high esteem if he sees your commitment in the form of hard work.

Conclusion: Show that you work hard. You don't need to run into the Red's office every five minutes, informing him that last night you stayed at work until half past eleven—he might not even be impressed. He might just ask you whether such a trifling little task like that warranted the time you spent on it. But you should report back regularly about what you have done and present—briefly—the result of your efforts.

Be willing to take initiative. Offer suggestions that the Red didn't ask for. As usual, get ready for a fight, but he will like that you are driven.

Please note the wording in the preceding sentence. It doesn't say that he'll like *you* because you are driven. It says "like that you *are* driven." A Red boss may very well like you—that's sometimes the case—but don't expect lots of glowing and pleasant praise.

How to Behave When You Meet a Red

You don't have to completely adapt to how Reds want you to behave—that would be surrendering. There are several other things you need to keep an eye on in order to achieve the results you want. Because Reds have their faults and failings but often turn a blind eye to them, you can help to achieve a better result if you know how. Here are some points to keep in mind.

"Details . . . Booooooring . . ."

Essentially, Reds dislike getting into details. It's boring and takes time. Thus, Reds tend to be careless about small matters. You can accuse Reds of many things, but meticulousness isn't typically one of them. For them the destination will always be more important than the journey, so Reds will do just about anything to achieve the desired results. Reds won't naturally stop to consider the small things or analyze their method.

Conclusion: If you really want to help Reds do better work, try to demonstrate the benefits of keeping an eye on the details. Explain that the results will be better and profits larger if they just consider a couple of small but crucial elements of the project.

Be prepared for the huff and puff and a general unwillingness to act on your advice. But if you're good at arguing, your advice will be followed. As we know, Reds are good at pushing themselves to the limit, just as long as they make headway.

Quick but Often Frightfully Wrong

As I have written several times before, everything in a Red's world is usually very urgent. You can figure out for yourself the risks this entails. Putting the pedal to the metal may seem like a good idea, but only when everything else, and most of all every*one* else, is on the same train. Normally, Reds rush ahead of the group, only to get annoyed when others can't keep pace.

A Red needs someone who can get him to pause and realize that not everyone has grasped the situation as quickly as he has. He'll never be able to carry out all the phases of a project on his own—even if he believes he can and probably will attempt to. He still needs to have his team with him.

You've probably heard the expression "quick and wrong."

Conclusion: Give examples of instances where time was lost by being too hasty. Point out the risks involved in hurrying too much. Explain that others can't keep up, and point out that it would be great if everyone knew what the project was about. Don't give in. Assert that not even he can manage everything himself. Force a Red to wait for others.

Afterwards, try to discuss the event and show clearly and distinctly what was gained and how much the Red has profited by taking things a bit slower.

"Let's Try a Few Completely Untested Ideas and See How It Goes."

Should we really do that? Red individuals aren't anxious about risks. Many Reds actively search for risky situations just for the thrill of it. In fact, what others might perceive as dangerous behavior a Red wouldn't even think of as risky. "Hey, life is risky. You won't get out of it alive!"

However, Reds do need someone who can weigh the advantages against the disadvantages. Disadvantages are boring, of course, so a Red individual will often simply ignore them. Since the answer to what risks you take often lies in the details, your approach should be similar to the way you handle discussing details with a Red.

Conclusion: Reds calculate risks by constantly looking at the facts. Facts are something they understand. Since Reds prefer not to look backwards—old and tiring—and focus on the present and the future, a plain and honest exchange of experiences may be called for.

Give examples of situations that historically were shown to be dangerous. It can be about business risks, going downhill skiing without a helmet, or calling the boss an idiot. Prove things with facts and demand that the person thinks twice before deciding to take on a new project without first having checked the conditions.

As usual: You're right—stick to your guns and don't give in.

"I'm Not Here to Be Your Pal. Or Anyone Else's, for That Matter."

Since many Reds are less relationally focused, they're frequently criticized for insisting that all relationships must take place on their terms, even in private life.

People around Reds frequently feel that they're being steamrolled by their friends or coworkers. It's rarely the Red's real intention; it's just something that happens. You can't make an omelet without breaking eggs, and so on.

Reds may not understand that others are avoiding them because they would rather avoid conflict. This also means that Reds can be excluded from important information. They may not feel excluded if they're invited for a beer on Friday evening, but it's far worse for them to feel left out of important decisions. In the worst case, this can lead them to suspect the people around them are deliberately withholding important information. The power struggle is just moments away.

Conclusion: Reds need to understand that the road to full transparency is to adapt to others. That thought may never even have crossed their minds; they're mostly focused on themselves and their own thing. But by realizing that no one can manage everything alone, they can be prevailed upon to pause and actually care about other people.

When a Red understands that many people think it's important to chat about their child's first tooth, how the cabin they rented on vacation was furnished, and about the boat they're dreaming of buying, he can listen actively and contribute to the discussion. Once a Red understands what all this small talk is about, the door is open. You may even learn something about him.

"What Kind of Weaklings Are You? Just Handle It!"

Reds just get angry. It can't be said any clearer than that. Their temperament is such that it detonates every now and then, causing migraines for everyone around. They don't notice it happening themselves; screaming a little bit is just another way to communicate.

No one likes a bully, but not everyone is willing to say so. When a Red tramples on someone's toes, you must tell him nicely that it doesn't work like that. He'll put on an innocent face and pretend that he doesn't understand what you're talking about. Secretly he'll be thinking that if some people are afraid of him, well, that's just tough.

Conclusion: You should confront his behavior immediately. Don't allow any exceptions; just say loudly and clearly that you won't tolerate coarse remarks, nastiness, and uncalled-for tantrums. Demand adult behavior, and if he loses his temper just leave the room. It's important that you never let him get his way just by barking his head off.

Just remember that this is a technique—bickering and brawling—that has worked for the Red for many years. As a child, he might have gotten his way by quarreling. More than likely, his family experienced his explosive temperament in his very early years. And you can bet that they just succumbed to avoid the air-raid siren. Very few people have confronted him about this, meaning that the demand for calmer conversations could easily lead to even louder protests. The one thing a Red detests more than anything else is being told that he must lower his voice.

Adapting to Yellow Behavior

What a Yellow Expects of You
"ISN'T IT NICE BEING HERE ALL TOGETHER?"

In essence, Yellows are not afraid of conflict. If something goes wrong, they can really blow a gasket, but if possible, they prefer a pleasant and cozy atmosphere. Yellows are at their best when everyone is being friendly and the sun is shining.

A Yellow, however, can be very sensitive to whether people are in good spirits or not. If the people in a group are in bad spirits and aggression is pouring down like from a cloudburst, he won't be happy at all.

Conclusion: A Yellow functions best when he is happy and content. His creativity is at its zenith and all his positive energy flows. You should strive to create a warm and friendly atmosphere around him.

Smile a lot, have fun, and laugh. Listen to his crazy jokes, laugh along at all his childish remarks, and kindle the easygoing and happy-go-lucky atmosphere.

If you do that, he'll feel better about you and listen to you more, which is always a good thing. A Yellow in a bad mood is not much fun to be with.

"I ASKED SOMEONE TO FIX THAT TINY DETAIL—I CAN'T REMEMBER WHO, THOUGH."

Keeping a Yellow's interest is, in all honesty, not the easiest thing to do. There are many things that bore the socks off a Yellow employee, customer, friend, or neighbor. A foolproof method to put a Yellow to sleep quickly and efficiently is to bring up lots of details.

Don't do that. A Yellow simply can't cope with details. It just gets boring. Not only will he forget what you're talking about, but he'll also simply think that he doesn't need any of those details. His strength lies in the broad brushstrokes. You can easily ask a Yellow to draw up a vision for the next ten years, but don't ask him to explain how to make it happen.

Conclusion: If you want to keep a Yellow's attention, strip away as much of the minutia as you possibly can. Always start with the big questions. It's perfectly fine that you know how to install the latest surround sound system, but don't tire your Yellow friend with it. It's not for him. He just wants to know how to get the music started.

It's just like with Reds, if not worse. Yellows don't care about *how* things work, only *that* they work. So put away the instruction manual—they'll never open it.

FOLLOW YOUR GUT. IT WORKS EVERY TIME.

If I had a dollar for every time a Yellow has explained a totally crazy decision by saying that it felt right, I could be sleeping at the Ritz. There's a study that shows that some people make better decisions if they only go on gut feeling. Whatever you do, never mention that to your Yellow friend or you'll never hear the end of it.

It must feel right. A Yellow can readily ignore the actual facts so long as it feels right. Don't misunderstand this: A Yellow understands perfectly well that some people look at facts and that this is important. He's not stupid. It's just that he's not interested. He wants to feel his way.

Do you want to get a Yellow to make a decision? Try to put the Excel spreadsheets aside, lean forward, and say with a broad smile, "How does this feel?"

He will understand exactly. And you'll get an answer.

Conclusion: Just accept that a Yellow feels his way. He has a high tolerance for uncertainty and isn't overly afraid of risks. Adapt to it. You can get through to him by showing him that you too follow your gut. No matter how wrong this might feel to you, this is the way to a Yellow's heart. He'll recognize himself in you. You'll become the best of friends. The sun will shine on you.

"THIS CAR IS A PROTOTYPE? THE CONCEPT COMPLETELY UNTESTED? NO ONE HAS EVER DONE THIS BEFORE? PERFECT!"

While a Red focuses on speed, a Yellow focuses on the latest and greatest. "New" is synonymous with "good." All Yellows know that. And why not? Without creativity and new inventions all development would simply grind to a halt, right?

Everyone likes having a little excitement in their everyday life. The difference lies in how we define "exciting." For a Yellow, "new" means "exciting." Yellows are so-called early adopters, the very first to try out new things. Check out who is wearing the latest fashion, who is the first to drive a new and preferably unusual model of car. Who has the latest cell phone and who knows what restaurant will be the newest sensation in a few months?

How can they keep track of all this? Don't ask me. They probably devote some of their time at work to keep au courant on all things new and interesting. But they're also early in implementing new work methods and new concepts to sell goods and services. It's just great fun.

Conclusion: Allow a Yellow to devote himself to the latest thing. He'll love it. If you want to sell something to a Yellow, use expressions like "state-of-the-art," "newly developed," and "never before used." Your potential customer will really get into gear.

"No one else has ever tried this? I have to have it!"

He'll like you because you're so exciting and so interesting and, above all, innovative. Equip yourself with lots of energy, because it can be challenging to keep up-to-date, but Yellows will adore you. However, be prepared to be replaced rather quickly if they find someone else who is even more knowledgeable about newer things.

"YOU SEEM INTERESTING. WANNA KNOW WHO I AM?"

By now we've established that Yellows like other people. They function best if they surround themselves with a crowd. Of course, Yellows don't like everyone they meet, but they will give the majority a decent chance.

You need to show a Yellow that you are just as open and friendly as he is. If you're way too closed and private, he'll feel unwelcome. Why didn't you reply when he spoke to you? Why didn't you smile at the funny story about his dog? Why doesn't he know anything about you? What are your dreams? Insufficient personal connection can result in a strong sense of insecurity, and your relationship won't develop in a positive direction. If you're Red or Blue, you need to think carefully about how to get this to work. If you want to, of course.

Conclusion: Become approachable. Demonstrate that you're available; smile a lot; be sure to have open body language. When a Yellow wonders where you grew up, don't just respond with "New York." Say that you lived in Chelsea, and that you loved jogging along the High Line, and that a pickpocket stole your wallet once while you were walking down Fifth Avenue, and that you met the love of your life when she accidentally dropped a plate of fries on your pants at a restaurant. It may seem a bit unnecessary, but you should definitely show interest in the Yellow as a person. Admittedly, it won't be difficult to find out things about him, because he'll freely tell you a great deal. But be sure to show that you are curious and interested.

And remember that Yellows are very susceptible to flattery.

How to Behave When You Meet a Yellow

To keep a Yellow in good spirits, you need to rub him the right way. The problem will become obvious after a while. They won't get that much work done. I've looked at a group of Yellows who were trying to solve a problem. They all spoke at the same time and had a great time, and when you asked them how things were going they said, "Fantastic!" But nothing got written down. To really make headway with Yellows, you need to do more than just create a great atmosphere. Once you've tuned into their frequency, you need to do the following.

Learn to Tell Whether a Yellow Is Actually Listening

I'm just going to say it like it is—Yellows are, beyond the shadow of a doubt, the worst listeners. Usually, they will never admit it. The very expression itself—"awful listeners"—is something negative, and they'll do anything to avoid negativity. Many Yellows really see themselves as good listeners. Who knows where they got that idea? It's simply not true. Of course, there are Yellows who listen—when it suits them. Or when they've already gotten what they wanted out of a conversation. But in most cases, forget about it.

They don't want to listen. They want to talk. Yellows simply think that they can express everything far better than anyone else. The problem is that they neglect to listen to what anyone else is saying.

Conclusion: When you're dealing with Yellows, there are certain things you need to do. It doesn't matter if you're speaking to your partner about your summer vacation or to a colleague about an ongoing project, you need a plan of action. You need to have prepared yourself carefully. You have to know what your message is and exactly what response you need from them. You must persuade the Yellow, happy person to answer your questions very concretely and hear him say, "Yes, I will be there at four just as I promised," or, "Of course I'll notify the customer exactly what we have agreed to."

But—big but—be prepared to follow up if it's important, because the Yellow didn't write down any of it. Unless you managed to persuade him to write it on his calendar, of course. That would be the best way. But in all other contexts, you should expect that what you've said has gone in one ear and out the other.

Learn How to Respond to "No Problem—That Won't Take Long at All!"

Yellows are optimists regarding time; that's just the way it is. Sure, your work can be done quickly, but rarely as quickly as a Yellow thinks. This has to do with the fact that he simply can't plan or structure his life. I've personally worked with people who legitimately believed that they could manage eight meetings per day, who thought that it only took two days to renovate an entire kitchen and that it is possible to walk across Manhattan in twenty minutes.

These are typical manifestations of a Yellow's optimism. The problem is obvious. It's impossible to accomplish everything a Yellow wants to do, particularly because he doesn't even know how long anything takes. And even if he does ask someone how long it takes, he doesn't listen to what the person says, because what he's saying is wrong. After all, the Yellow believes he probably knows best.

The other problem is that he won't get into gear when he should. Do you know anyone who has taken a day off to paint the bedroom and at three o'clock in the afternoon, hasn't opened the can of paint yet? "I'll just do this first, then call so and so, then pop out for a bit, then . . ." Sometimes I wonder if the people who schedule the subways are all Yellow. There's nothing nasty in this; it's just about a total inability to have a realistic sense of time. And a genuine belief that this commodity is inexhaustible.

I remember a dinner I went to with a few Yellow friends. The pub had a policy of ninety-minute reservations, which meant that if you got there twenty-five minutes late there wouldn't be time for an appetizer or for dessert because the kitchen couldn't manage it in time. My partner and I arrived fifteen minutes early—we both have some splashes of Blue in our profiles. We went to the table and sat down to wait for the others. Time passed. Forty minutes later, twenty-five minutes late, they arrived, joyfully joking about how they had forgotten the time. We managed to order just a main course, eat it, and quickly pay for it before the next guest wanted his table. The strange thing was that when we spoke about the incident afterwards, their recollection was that they were just a few minutes late. They had simply repressed the fact that they missed 30 percent of the dinner.

Conclusion: Coordinate all appointments properly with Yellows. Synchronize your watches. Explain very clearly that the plane takes off at 8:00 P.M. and that if he doesn't show up by then he'll be left standing at the gate. Say it like it is: If he's not in his car outside your door two hours before the plane takes off, you'll drop down dead of a heart attack. Tell the Yellow that you will be deeply irritated with him and that your friendship could be damaged due to his continual slipups.

If the dinner is due to start at 7:00 P.M., invite everyone for that time, but make it 6:30 for your Yellow friends. They'll arrive last anyway. They'll come with very well-worded excuses. Be prepared for very colorful stories. But also know that Yellows will emphatically deny that they are optimists regarding time. They'll insist that they most certainly kept an eye on the clock. It was just that something happened on the way.

It Looks Like a Hand Grenade Went Off in Here

The most cluttered desks I have ever seen have all belonged to Yellows. Computer screens with so many Post-it notes stuck to them that you can barely see the screen. The most topsy-turvy garages and the most overloaded attics belong to Yellows as well. But this is only the visible. Ask to look at a Yellow person's calendar. Or handbag. Don't even think about looking in a Yellow's closet. And this is still only the purely physical.

Meetings are moved or forgotten; things disappear; whole cars are lost in parking lots. Keys are gone without a trace. Furthermore, many Yellows have no ability to plan their day. They can go to the supermarket five times in a row and buy three things at a time because they didn't write down what they needed. This can be because they don't know what they want until they get there or because they're sure they'll be able to recall the nineteen things they need to buy. (Yellows have a very generous view of their own ability. They'll tell anyone who wants to listen that they have the best memory in the world.)

Conclusion: If you really want to help a Yellow get organized, make sure he gets at least some structure in his life. Help out by creating a simple list. If you are going shopping: Write down everything yourself. Your partner or pal will forget half of the items.

Create a structure for him. Yellows are the ones who are most in need of structure in the form of diagrams and checklists. Paradoxically, they hate all of that. They won't let themselves be "shoehorned" into a system not of their own choosing. Be diplomatic. If you press too hard, you can get some powerful reactions:

"Why does everything have to be micromanaged? Are we living in a fascist state, or what?"

Remember That for Yellows the Most Important Thing Is to Look Good. All the Time.

"Me, me, me." Yellows have strong egos, just like Reds, no doubt about that. They like getting attention; they throw themselves into the center of things faster than anyone else. They enjoy themselves the most when they're in the middle of where the action is. Your yellow friend is a ray of sunshine, talking louder and faster than everyone else and lighting up a room with his behavior.

"Shine all the spotlight on me. See me, hear me, like me." But this means that no one else gets any space. Many conversations end up with the Yellow individual loudly and resonantly speaking about his experience or his opinion. No matter what you are talking about—war, starvation, dieting, cars, executives, gardens—a Yellow will bring up a story in which he himself is the protagonist. If he doesn't have any story, he'll make one up.

Their thoughts often begin with the word "I." "I want," "I think," "I can," "I know," "I will." It's quite natural. They like other people, but there is one thing they like even more: themselves.

Conclusion: Yellows need to understand that there are other people in the room or working on the project besides themselves. You can never allow Yellows to consume all the oxygen. They need to hear—

from someone with courage and perseverance—that they have to let others enter the conversation or whatever it may be.

It's impossible to explain this in the midst of a conversation with others present. It won't fall on fertile ground. A Yellow can be very offended by such criticism. He'll think things like, "Everyone else just thinks of themselves," or, "I'm the only one who looks out for me." This type of feedback must be given discreetly and in a positive way. It depends a little bit on how Yellow the person in question is, so you will probably need a plan.

Be prepared for one thing: You may very well become enemies in the process. You're definitely taking a risk here. Hearing that you are egocentric and self-centered is extremely unflattering. Yellows will understand this; they're not stupid. But they will just think that your analysis is wrong. So you'll have to work a lot here. Or swap pals.

All Talk, but No Walk

I might as well get straight to the point here to avoid confusion: Yellows talk more than they work. They have a penchant for talking about everything they need to do rather than actually doing anything. Everyone who knows a genuine Yellow knows exactly what I'm talking about.

Okay, so many people have trouble getting motivated to work, especially with boring tasks. But Yellows find it particularly hard to leave the starting block when faced with uncomfortable tasks. It may be about having to call a dissatisfied customer, or getting an oil change, or going to the pharmacy. If it's dull and uninspiring, it won't happen. Their excuses for avoiding these tasks will be numerous and imaginative.

Because a Yellow's perspective on time is based in the future, they spend more time talking about the future than dedicating their energy to getting there. Seldom have so many crazy plans been drawn up or so many insane goals set as is done by Yellows. Because they think aloud, people around them believe that these fantasies are going to happen: "Wow! It sounds amazing!"

Conclusion: To help your Yellow friend you need to make sure that he puts his shovel in the ground and starts digging. Push him, but push gently. Treat him a little bit like you would treat a child. Be kind but clear. If he notices that you're becoming his taskmaster, things may become difficult. Yellows hate feeling controlled. They need the most help to get into gear, but that doesn't mean they like it. They are free souls and don't obey anyone else.

So you need to be diplomatic. Softly and gently explain the value of actually doing the job itself, now that he knows what needs to be done. Take a moment to explain to a Yellow how the great popularity he already enjoys can actually be increased even further if he just happens to get finished. Everyone will love him, and he will be more beloved than ever.

Does that sound simple? It *is* simple. All you need to do is overcome your resistance to inflating someone's ego in such an obvious way. But it will work.

Realize That Yellows May See Your Lips Moving but Not Hear Anything You're Saying

This could very well be a subtitle to a section on bad listeners, because these things are connected to each other. All of us make mistakes and no one is perfect. This is obvious to everyone, even to a Yellow. In hypothetical discussions, Yellows can agree that other people really need to get a grip, sort things out, and do better. They can even admit that there are no perfect people. So far, no problems. The problems arise when we try to make a particular Yellow understand that *he* may need to improve. This creates a conflict, especially if the criticism is expressed in public.

Yellow people find it difficult to cope with criticism. They don't like it because it doesn't make them look good. Imagine, there's someone who doesn't like everything they do and everything they say! I have individually sat down with Yellows and given them personal feedback on their profiles. Everything goes fine until we get to the page with the heading "Areas of Improvement," which is to say, weaknesses.

Even if we're on good terms, the temperature in the room gets significantly cooler. Defensive walls pop up quicker than you can say "poor self-awareness." Deep down the Yellow individual knows that he has weaknesses; he just won't consider talking about them.

Conclusion: If you wish to get through to a Yellow with negative feedback, you need to be persistent. Create a friendly atmosphere in the room and find the right tone so that your criticism lands where it should.

You can always slam your fist on the table as hard as you can to really shake him up, lay down the cold, hard truth, and give it to him straight. I don't recommend this. Better to work slowly and consistently, repeating the same feedback until he understands.

Clarity is key. Make sure to be extremely well prepared, with all possible facts to substantiate your claims. Yellows are clever manipulators. If he senses that you're not serious in your criticism and that you won't follow up, he'll lure you off track. He is good at smokescreens. Make sure you don't get lost in the fog.

Get real answers to your questions, and be sure that he understands the message. Insist that he writes down what you have said. Ask him to repeat your feedback.

You also need to set up a plan of action. But save that for the next meeting. Right now, you've probably gotten as far as you can with a Yellow. You'll just exhaust yourself if you keep going.

One more thing: This doesn't happen with positive feedback. Then, the Yellow will jump on the bandwagon quicker than you can imagine.

Adapting to Green Behavior

What a Green Expects of You
EVERYTHING SHOULD FEEL GOOD ALL THE TIME

Security will always be important to a Green. A Green worries about everything that may happen. He doesn't like insecurity and solves it by hiding under the covers. If you don't see it, then it's not there. He doesn't want to be anywhere if it's too insecure. He strives for stability and doesn't even want to think about wild gambles.

You may be thinking, The world is a dangerous place to live. There's an infinite number of dangers out there. Absolutely anything can go wrong. My relationship may fall apart; I might get sick; my husband [or wife] could leave me; my children might think I am an idiot. I can lose my job; my boss may start agreeing with my children; I could end up in conflict with a lot of people. On the way to work, I could have a car accident. A person can die from a tiny fish bone caught in his throat!

All these things make life scary. Anything can happen. Many Greens I've known over the years in my role as a coach have said that all these potential dangers paralyze them. They become overwhelmed with thoughts about these risks and dangers. They become completely powerless to act. And since they're not particularly motivated to get out in the world, it becomes easier to just stay at home. Nice and safe at home by the hearth.

It wasn't Greens who left their homes and immigrated to America. They would never have gotten on the boat, because who knows how the trip would go? And if you survived the voyage itself, who could really say what you would find when you got there? Those stories about all those people who achieved success and wealth could well be humbug from start to finish. And if you did get a job and if you did find somewhere to live, who knows if you would be happy? Imagine if you end up even more miserable than you were at home! You know what you have, but you have no idea at all what you'll get.

Conclusion: Accept that this person doesn't think like you do. Accept that he is driven just as much by fear as by anything else—perhaps even more. Show that you're prepared to listen to what he is anxious about. Don't say things like "There's nothing to be afraid of." It doesn't work because the fear itself is real. And it's also not true. There are many legitimate things to be afraid of. We all have things we're anxious about; a Green just has more of them.

Instead, help your Green friend to face his fear of the unknown. Encourage him to brave things that feel scary and still move ahead. Just as we learned to swim as children, despite the fact that the water looked cold and dangerous, you can give support through small, gentle nudges forward.

When your friend says that the grass only *looks* greener on the other side, simply take a deep breath and keep at it.

NOTHING HAPPENED. TWICE.

I'm sure you recall that I mentioned the Green's passivity. Nothing is too big to be ignored. Being proactive and driven, having an active lifestyle—all these things disturb tranquility. And it won't be appreciated. He won't be happy if you're constantly coming up with new things to do.

Greens feel better when they don't have to be active. They come home on a Friday evening so completely exhausted from spending the week trying to accomplish as little as possible that they now need to take a good rest. I've met Greens whose efforts to avoid work cost them more energy than actually doing the work.

The consequences are obvious to those around them. They don't like weekends with full schedules. Visiting the mother-in-law, organizing a picnic, taking his son to soccer, cleaning out the garage, inviting the neighbors over for dinner—everything becomes a burden for him, and half the time nothing gets done at all. A Green glides under the radar and disappears completely. He needs peace and quiet to be able to do what he does best. Peace and quiet make him feel safe and content.

Conclusion: It's important to respect this on one level. We need to put ourselves in other people's shoes, knowing how stressful it can be for them to be constantly on the go. In today's society, it's not possible to avoid all the bustle and activity. It means that a genuine Green often feels that he is doing something wrong. He hears about everyone else's weekends, their activities, how they've completed one complicated project after the other. For a Green that just sounds exhausting.

The solution is to allow the Green his periods of peace, quiet, and inactivity. He needs to function like that. This doesn't mean, of course, that he can sit on his butt his whole life, but he does need to be allowed to do a reasonable amount of—nothing.

"WHERE ARE WE GOING? I THINK I'LL SIT THIS ONE OUT. . ."

Stability and predictability are valuable to a Green. And when you think about it, it's very logical—it's a good thing knowing what's going to happen. We probably all have some measure of control dependency. We simply want to know. For Greens, this dependency is very strong. When Reds ask what, Yellows wonder who. When Blues ask why, Greens want to know how.

A Green simply needs to know what the plan is. What needs to happen? When will things be taking place? What should he expect?

Just look at how it works at home. Who always has the same spot at the breakfast table? I know that many of us are creatures of habit, but if you snitch a Green's since-a-long-time-ago-claimed chair, you unhinge his very existence and he won't be able to get his food down.

But their need for predictability goes further than that. It's about anything that even resembles change. In our society today, the only thing that's permanent is change. Nothing is totally predictable; everything rotates on its own axis and appears in new shapes and forms. And all of this is extremely stressful for Greens.

Conclusion: Since a Green won't come up with anything on his own, it will be you and I who will have to handle the planning. But maybe that's okay. We can help ease Greens' minds by explaining every step of the plan. Instead of just saying that I've invited guests over for the weekend, I could explain that we will be having John and Mary over for dinner and we'll be offering a three-course dinner consisting of an appetizer, a main course, and a dessert. I'll fix the main course while my Green partner should make the dessert and should follow this recipe. I explain who is doing what. Who will buy the wine, who will buy the flowers, and so on. I might even explain which day my Green partner has to do the shopping. And who knows, maybe I'll write down the address of the flower shop with a list of exact instructions about what should be purchased.

Does this sound exaggerated? Not at all. Remember, Greens aren't world champions at taking their own initiative. Think of your family as a company—everyone doesn't do the same things, because we're good at different things. If you're better at taking the initiative, do it. But make sure that your Green partner is on board. Otherwise, there's a risk that he'll run out the back door.

How to Behave When You Meet a Green

Okay, now you know how your Green friends would like to be handled. The result will be a calm and excellent relationship, and you will be good friends for many years. Nice, huh? But you can't stop there, because unless you're a genuine Green yourself you'll want to actually do something every now and then. And you'll need to have some appropriate strategies to kick-start your stability-loving friend.

"Why Does Everything Have to Be Such a To-do? Ugh. I'm Going to Bed."

I've said this before, but we need to spill more ink on this issue. Greens don't like friction of any kind. They back off when a discussion heats up or if you frown at the wrong time. Everything could be a potential conflict, and this is a very bad condition for all Greens. They lock themselves in and become silent and passive.

Many years ago, I was giving a sales conference at which I trained sellers in personal effectiveness. One of them was playing with his cell phone unremittingly, and when I—nicely and gently—asked him to write his text messages during the break, he completely stiffened up and stopped speaking. He didn't respond to any questions or take part in any discussions. He didn't so much as lift his pen for the remainder of the day. He glared at me, and when I asked what the problem was he just shrugged his shoulders.

He gave me what is probably the worst evaluation I have ever received. Although the conference was five days long, it was that one day that was critical to him, and he truly cut me to shreds. He had never encountered such a rude and incompetent consultant. He felt as if I had stuck a knife in his back. Obviously, this was a completely unreasonable reaction, especially considering that we had agreed not to use our mobile phones during work sessions. But it didn't matter—this guy still thought that I had wronged him wholly and entirely, and he punished me the only way he could: through total passivity. I phoned him afterwards and confronted him about it. He admitted that it was juvenile behavior and apologized.

Conclusion: If you have a comment to make about a Green's behavior, make sure you're careful about how you present it. For example, if it involves criticism, you should deliver it in private. Make sure that the person you are talking to understands that you still like him, but that you believe that he and the group (work team, sports team, family, association) will function better if he changes certain things. Don't ask him what he can do about the behavior; just ask him to do certain specific things. It may be that he knows what to do, but as usual, he will not lead the conversation—you'll need to do that.

"It Was Better Before. Much Better."

When I'm talking about change, one of my favorite exercises is to ask everyone in the group who is afraid of change to stand up. Occasionally someone will stand up, but it's more common that no one moves.

Why? Because we all understand that change is inevitable and necessary if we're going to keep up with the world. Some people can admit that they dislike change, but this observation is only at an intellectual level. And so we all sit quietly in our seats pretending that there are no opponents to change to be found here. And besides, no one else is standing up.

After that, my second question is, "Who thinks that someone else in the group is afraid of change?" Suddenly the whole group stands up, and they look around quite amused. So who doesn't like change? Answer: "Everyone else. And because those other people are the problem, I don't need to do anything at all."

The issue is widespread. The majority of the population has Green as its dominant quality. This is the main reason why we can't accept change with open arms. Everything new is evil, and it should be strongly discouraged.

Rapid change is the most difficult to accept. The faster it is, the worse it is. So the faster the wheels of society spin, the more frantic all those opponents of change become. We see this all the time in new reports. Yellows and Reds devise constant change, Greens and Blues, who are in the majority, try to keep up. And the stress just increases.

Conclusion: If you want Greens to accept change, you'll have to equip yourself with a good dollop of patience. Break down the process into small pieces and set aside a few weeks to persuade, win over, and spell out the particulars. You must describe the process in detail, and since no one is going to take any notes, you'll have to go through it again, and again, and again until the message gets home.

The group must get the chance to feel its way to the only possible solution—change. Once that feeling has developed, you're home free. But the road is long and complicated. You need to know exactly where you're heading, and you need to remind yourself constantly why you are going through all this trouble. If you are Red, every day you'll be seized by the urge to simply force your opinion on the group, but I hardly need to explain that you might as well shut the company down if you do that. It would spare everyone involved a great deal of time and suffering.

Someone Needs to Take the Helm If We Aren't Going to Sink to the Bottom

Let's be honest—isolated from everything else Green behavior is not a distinct leadership quality. Especially because oftentimes leadership is all about change. Fortunately, this doesn't mean that there are no good Green bosses—there are many of them out there—but they don't grow on trees. They won't step forward in the same way as Reds and Yellows do.

It's convenient not to have to take responsibility. I think all of us have a certain degree of laziness in us. It's liberating not to have to think, to avoid having to decide and just be a passenger. Of course, it varies depending on the circumstances, but Greens have developed this laziness into an art form. They don't want any responsibility because a) it can lead to conflict if someone doesn't agree with a decision or b) there may be lots of extra work and that's never good. And so they dodge it, for as long as possible.

Responsibility is burdensome, requiring inner strength as well as an external drive to assume it. But at the same time, it's a measure of maturity, and it begins with taking responsibility for yourself and your own life. Greens (and some other colors on occasion) have a tendency to blame everything and everyone but themselves. I knew a woman who had an entire list of things she could blame if something didn't go her way. She blamed the government, the opposition, taxation, her employer, the state of the market, her education, her parents, her husband, and her children. Sometimes it was the weather's fault. She blamed everything and everyone except herself.

What did she gain from this? She didn't have to take any responsibility herself. Because there was always some other factor that was responsible for this and that, she never had to tackle her own problems and really change anything. I remember that I asked her to explain how it was possible that she was also not on her own list, but I suspect that she didn't understand the question.

Given the monumental passivity a Green person can demonstrate, we immediately end up with problems. If someone doesn't row the boat or take the helm, no amount of prayer will ever help. And Greens will remain seated, waiting for help. (Usually, someone comes and helps out; so, despite everything, they survive.)

Conclusion: If you want to make headway with a large group of Greens, you have to take command, get a firm hold on the steering wheel, and, in some cases, simply get into the driver's seat yourself. Asking a group of Greens to solve a task is as much use as trying to put a brake on a canoe. They won't get started unless you put them on the track.

A doggone-I-thought-they-were-adults approach will not work. Sure, they're adults, but they're children when it comes to such basic things like making decisions. This is because once upon a time they made a decision not to make any decisions. So someone has to put his foot down and just decide.

Do it and do it now. But at the same time, do it gently. . .

Adapting to Blue Behavior

What a Blue Expects of You
IT'S BEST TO THINK EVERYTHING ALL THE WAY THROUGH FROM THE BEGINNING

A Blue prepares meticulously. If you've planned to meet at a certain place at a certain time, you can rest assured that he'll be there. A Blue will have gone through all the material, analyzed everything down to the smallest detail, and he'll be prepared to discuss just about anything on the topic. He will have an alternative plan and a contingency plan for that as well.

HE'S THOUGHT OF EVERYTHING, SO YOU SHOULD, TOO

Being Blue is a little like doing military service: No excuses will be allowed. If you get a flat tire, you should be prepared for it. If there's a puncture in the spare tire, you must have a plan for that, too. A Blue will have some critical questions if you say something like "That's just the way it is." The next time you meet him, his confidence in you will be tarnished.

Conclusion: Make sure you can show that you've done your homework and are well prepared. For example, when a Blue customer or policy maker has a question you should be able to pull out that exact folder from your briefcase. Don't make a big deal out of knowing the answer. He expected nothing less.

And—most important—if you don't have the answer, just say so. Acknowledge that you don't know. Don't offer any excuse just to get out of the situation. When the Blue discovers the white lie—and he will—you will fall out of favor. It's not ideal to have to come back with the answer the next day, but it's definitely preferable to telling a fib.

A car salesman I know usually says that when he meets Blue customers he knows from the outset that the customer is more informed about a particular model of car than he, since as a seller he might have fifty models to keep track of. Blue customers don't ask questions to find things out; they ask to confirm what they already know. So the car salesman doesn't even try to pretend anymore. If he doesn't know the answer, he acknowledges it and then finds out. It's the only way to win a Blue customer's confidence.

WE'RE NOT HERE TO HANG OUT AND BE COZY

This is a given if we're referring to a working relationship. Stick to the job. Make sure to stay focused on the task at hand. A Blue is not at all interested in your personal preferences or what you think about his choice of car, house, sport, or anything else that is not related to work. He's there to work. Period.

I remember once that after about five or six meetings with a personnel manager in a big company I thought I had gotten to know him. We had passed the stage of shaking hands every time, and by now he knew how I preferred my coffee. At the seventh visit it occurred to me to ask him what he planned to do over the holidays. I don't know what came over me. At first his look became vacant and then his anxious eyes began to wander all over the room. I ended up saying some nonsense to cover up my mistake. I hadn't told him what I had done on my holidays, either. About four visits later, he informed me gently that he planned to go to Thailand over the new year with his family.

That was the opening.

Conclusion: Stick to the task. Work with checklists where factual matters are noted—things you can tick off together with the Blue. If you're Yellow, put a part of your spontaneity aside. For that matter, put away as much spontaneity as you can. Force yourself to do one thing at a time. Remind yourself that a Blue will rarely or never ask how things are going or show interest in your personal problems. Don't ask how things are going for him on a personal level, either. The word itself would be his answer: "Personal. This is private. Stay off." In time he will open up if he wants to. It's not that he doesn't like you; he just wants to work first. Accept this and it will go well.

NO VISION NECESSARY. LET'S ALL STAY IN THE REAL WORLD, THANK YOU VERY MUCH.

Your Blue friends aren't flying around up there in the blue, blue sky. They're on the ground using their critical minds to judge whether things are realistic or not. While you may think they're boring, suspicious, or downright pessimistic, they believe that they're only realists. They want to know what reality looks like, not what the world looks like if you're a dreamer or a visionary.

I remember once when I was working in the banking world we were having a kickoff event and I wanted to inspire my team to do great things, the likes of which had never before been seen. I finished my rousing speech by exclaiming, "Soon we will stand on top of the peak of success and look down on the market we've conquered. We, all of us, will be atop that mountain!" While both Yellow and Red and, to a certain extent, Green employees smiled and were hyped up, the Blues only said one thing: "We can't imagine ourselves up there. How did we get up there?"

The Yellows shouted, "Don't you have any vision?"

And the Blues replied, "We have Excel."

If a plan seems crazy, a Blue will never have any confidence in it. There's no point in playing on his feelings or trying to promote ideas that are way too wild. What you say needs to have realistic perspectives; otherwise, you won't get anywhere.

Conclusion: Think through what you want to say and what you want to convince a Blue to believe. Put daydreams and visions aside. It may even be worth rethinking the kind of language you will use to talk about your plan. Skip all those inspirational speeches that Yellows and Reds adore. Stick to the facts, and be clear.

If you have an idea that hasn't been tested before, try to set reasonable goals. Don't say that you will dominate the market within three months or that the Little League team will win the championship despite having lost all of their matches so far. They'll only consider you a lunatic. If you have Yellow in your own profile, you should really think twice about how you interact with Blues. You're already fighting an uphill battle as far as a Blue is concerned. And be careful to avoid any overly dramatic body language.

DETAILS: FACTS ARE THE ONLY THINGS THAT MATTER

Details are essential to communicating with a Blue. If you really want to get through to them, you must make sure to be very exact. Carelessness or ignoring the details won't be appreciated.

More than one seller has been turned out of a sales visit due to negligence—for failing to know the nitty-gritty details. And remember that it's not a question of whether the details are crucial for a particular decision or not. They may have no real bearing on the issue at all. But a Blue decision maker simply wants to know.

He also wants to know *exactly*. If you're asked how much a particular product costs, don't say, "About ten dollars." Say, "Nine dollars and seventy-three cents." It's a precise answer. A Blue is more interested in an exact price than a low price. He may very well negotiate, but he wants to know the precise cost.

Conclusion: Prepare yourself well. When you think you're prepared and that you know all there is to know about an issue, go through it all one more time. Make sure you have answers to absolutely everything. Accept that this person might want to have more data to feel secure. Give him the details he needs in order to move on. He'll always wonder if there's any more information. But this way, you can keep him calm and, you hope, content.

THERE'S NO SUBSTITUTE FOR QUALITY

Quality is what drives a Blue. Everything else is secondary. Everything else he focuses on stems from a deeply rooted desire that everything must be perfect. A Blue is discontented if he's not allowed to perform his work to an exacting standard. It has nothing to do with what quality of work is actually needed. It's simply due to his belief that things must always be done the proper way.

This, of course, takes a huge amount of time. But the advantage is obvious—if you do it right from the beginning, you will avoid having to redo it. This is actually a great way of saving time. But since a Blue does not think in terms of hours, days, or even weeks—but rather in months and years—he doesn't see the potential downside of his exacting standards. If a thing is worth doing, it's worth doing right—and that takes time. It's as simple as that.

Conclusion: Be particularly meticulous in your work when trying to impress a Blue; otherwise, he will view you as sloppy and careless. You should be on your guard about expressing yourself using negative terms concerning how the Blue spends too much time just on quality. Use words like "careful control," "properly inspected," "the importance of quality." Avoid criticizing Blues for taking too much time or fussing over details that may be unnecessary. Instead, praise them for their attention to detail and the superior work they do. Let the Blue understand that you are doing quality work and that you understand its value.

This means that you should prepare very carefully before any meetings with a Blue. He judges you by the merit of the work you create. Not by how funny you are, not by who you know, not by whether or not you invite him to fancy lunches. None of this means anything if you are careless. When you are finished with a task—double-check it. If possible—triple-check. Have someone else look at it. Only then should you show it to your Blue colleague.

How to Behave When You Meet a Blue

Just agreeing to a Blue's initiative would be like driving a car with the parking brake on. Your task is most likely to get things moving, but you can't just hit the gas. Instead, you need to find the right lever to pull and take off the Blue parking brake.

A Blue has feelings like everyone else, and he appreciates people. It just looks a little different. Because most of a Blue's emotions are self-contained, he may seem a little cold. No facial expressions to speak of, no gestures, no emotional expressions at all. Blues often don't seem interested in other people and simply focus on the issue at hand.

If we're sitting in an accounting firm or if we're trying to solve an important problem in the company, then this is a good approach. But every time other people, especially Yellows or Greens, are involved, a Blue's tendency to dissociate from others can be problematic. He simply doesn't realize that other people don't function in the same way. People want to feel like they can relate to this person. They don't want to feel like robots.

Conclusion: Remind him that other people have feelings. Give examples of times when he bruised other people's feelings—like when he pointed out all the flaws in the neighbor's new house. Explain that he doesn't need to express himself critically all the time. Show him that people can take great offense when others criticize their home, car, spouse, or children. Be clear and tell him that being honest isn't an excuse for being callous and remind him that it isn't as simple as "saying things as they are." He didn't say things as they are. He only said what he thought or believed about a certain thing.

Point out that constant criticism rarely accomplishes anything. This won't be an easy task, because he will think that you are wrong. He has every right to criticize and point out errors and flaws. If he sees an error, he can't just ignore it. You might just have to tell him that he's being impossible.

The Devil's in the Details

Have you ever listened to a Blue tell an interesting story? Let's say he got a flat on the highway. He'll begin by saying that his alarm clock, a Sony, rang a minute earlier because it was Thursday and on Thursdays he gargles a little longer with Listerine—the green kind, since a taste test done by Consumers Union, the largest independent consumer-testing organization in the world, in their bulletin issued last March clearly demonstrated that it's preferable. Breakfast consisted of two seven-minute eggs and coffee. Nespresso has a new roast, but he didn't enjoy it. At least 9 percent of the beans were damaged, which made him reflect on how bean structure affects the mouthfeel of the coffee. Then he fetched the newspaper *The New York Times,* since they had made a special offer, 18 percent discount for three months. At the post office he spoke to his neighbor—who also reads *The New York Times*—about the best way to take care of the lawn in September. "There's an interesting website that discusses different types of autumn fertilizer, very fascinating. . . ."

Rome Wasn't Built in a Day!

Haste is only for sloppy people. We can tell Blues to hurry up, but it goes in one ear and out the other. Speed isn't an end in itself. Oftentimes, Blues slow down even more when they're feeling stress, since in a high-stakes situation you really don't have time to make mistakes. Better to be careful to avoid time-consuming fixes.

This may be true, but sometimes things are urgent, particularly in our fast-paced society—hurry to work, hurry at work, hurry home from the same job. Hurry in school, in traffic, in the supermarket—everywhere, everything is urgent. I don't encourage any form of behavior that may lead to stress-related illnesses. But sometimes you have to speed up in order to stay in the race. Outwardly, the Blue is quite unmoved. He works at his own pace without worrying that those around him may burn out from their more hectic pace. They actually have themselves to blame.

Conclusion: Calmly and methodically tell the Blue that next week he'll need to work at a faster pace. Explain exactly why this is so important. Establish that you have only forty-eight hours left to complete the project. This time is precious and must be used correctly. Point to the big picture. Give him valid reasons he should go against his instincts.

You can readily prove your point by highlighting the long-term plan: "We must stay on track or we'll miss our next deadline." If, for example, you're talking about renovating your house, it might be helpful to negotiate in advance when everything will be ready. If the in-laws are arriving in four weeks, then the house must be done by then no matter what. Calculate how many hours can be devoted to the renovations. Decide which activities should be given priority. Make sure the Blue sticks to his schedule and keeps moving forward once he's completed each task. Otherwise, the risk is that he will spend five hours polishing the finer details—time that he doesn't have.

If you have all the time in the world, well, that's another matter.

"If It's in the Book, It Must Be True."

"Can't we go by our gut feelings?" Try saying that to a strictly Blue individual and see what happens. Gut feeling is the opposite of rational thought, and nothing could be more foreign to the Blue.

Wait a minute: Does this mean that you should never use your own intuition if you're working with Blues? Even Blue individuals have what we call a sixth sense or "nose" for what can be right. The difference is that they don't trust it because it can, of course, be wrong. The problem is that it's impossible to prove anything with the help of gut feeling. The only thing that counts is the facts. And even the facts might not be enough—there may be more information out there that would change everything!

Conclusion: Tell your Blue friend that if he has to make a decision without all the facts, he can follow his gut. This can apply to work or ordering at a new restaurant. Speak clearly and loudly to the Blue, and explain that if he doesn't make a decision he'll end up going hungry. Prove that it's better to do something rather than remaining paralyzed, waiting for more information.

Point out that that it's logical to use intuition in this situation because you don't have all of the facts. Explain that the results will still be good—maybe just 95.3 percent of what they could be but still good. Help him to calculate risk but also to move on.

Decisions Made Here

Because the Blue experiences the decision itself as less important than the path to the decision, stagnation can occur. After painstakingly collecting facts and meticulously studying all available conditions, you finally come to the moment of truth—the decision. There is a risk that everything can deadlock. On the one hand . . . but on the other hand . . .

A project manager I met a few years ago wanted to buy a new car. For eight months he test-drove sixteen different makes. Over fifty different models in different combinations: different engines, bodies, transmissions, interiors, colors. He tried everything. Fabric versus leather upholstery. Gas versus diesel. Automatic versus manual. He did calculations on fuel consumption and depreciation and gave different graphs to respective car salesmen for an evaluation. After considerable internal torment, he bought a Volvo V70, then the country's most popular car, in metallic silver, the most popular color at that time. This particular model was the most tested car of all by the various consumer agencies that year. You would think he could have picked that car just by reading about it.

"Why did you go and buy the most common, boring car after all that research?" everyone asked. "Why not?" he replied.

You can help with a Blue's decision stagnation. Provide him with the crucial piece to the puzzle. Softly and gently, try to steer him in the right direction or, in any case, in *a* direction.

Conclusion: Pay attention to when the decision process stalls out. Suppose, for example, two equally strong candidates have applied for an opening at your company. So far, everything has gone well. The Blue decision maker has submitted detailed information via email and kept everyone informed about the necessary steps. The process has been followed to the letter.

In order to get something to happen, provide the decision maker with the necessary data required for him to make a decision about one of the candidates. Push him to make a choice. Remind him that the deadline is approaching. Point out the repercussions of delaying the decision—the quality of the company's work will suffer if he doesn't hire a new employee. Explain that everything has been properly considered and that, regardless of which candidate he chooses, all the risks have been eliminated.

In Conclusion

Now you have some basic information about how you can interact with the different colors so that you can get to where you want to go. The first step is to try to tune into the frequency of others and then adapt to them. In this way, you gain their trust and they are able to recognize themselves in you.

So the basic rule is to meet a Red with Red behavior, Yellow with Yellow, Green with Green, and finally Blue with Blue. You may think that it sounds simple. The difficulty comes, for example, if you are Yellow and must adapt to a Blue. You might need more training here. It depends on what color you are, how strong your self-awareness is, and how willing you are to make headway with a specific contact in your everyday life. You can always do what Adam did—you can continue being yourself.

The next step will be to start leading the person away from common pitfalls. As you have seen, each color has its obvious weaknesses. Here a Blue can help a Yellow become more concrete and the Yellow can perhaps persuade the Blue to loosen up and be a little more spontaneous.

At the risk of sounding clichéd—it's all about working together, about meeting one another in the middle. You already knew that, but now you know how to do it.

13

How to Deliver Really Bad News

The Challenge of Speaking Your Mind

Who looks forward to bad news? No one. And yet, every now and then, we still need to break some bad news. In the world around us, the unexpected can happen, and sometimes the lot falls to you to inform someone about something negative. Reds are the best at delivering news that no one wants to hear. Rather insensitively, they'll just come out and say that you've been fired, before asking you if you would like milk in your coffee. Tricky? No, not at all. He was just finished with the task at hand.

But there's a difference, of course, between bad news and *bad* news. It's one thing to convey a personal criticism and another to tell you that your grandmother has just died. The latter is always difficult, and no one will receive that news well. However, the former can be fine-tuned and adjusted in a way that makes it easier for someone to receive.

Feedback alone is a gigantic topic. It gives many people a stomachache just thinking about it, and many people I meet during my leadership programs find this area particularly difficult. Not only is it difficult to give feedback, but it also seems to be difficult to receive it. This is really strange, because the latter means just sitting there and listening. But anyone who has received some hard criticism and left the room afterwards knows that sometimes you can't utter a word. When delivered badly, it will leave you feeling sick.

The solution for many executives I meet seems be simply skipping giving any kind of feedback. We don't know how to give either positive or negative feedback, so we ignore it. I hardly need to point out why this isn't a good solution.

The Downside of Just Doing Your Job

Once, many years ago, I had a colleague, Micke, who was exceptionally good at his job. Of all of us, he was the one who always met his budget targets. He had won every sales contest and was held in high esteem by customers. Boxes of chocolates and bottles of wine would arrive for him from far and wide on a regular basis.

What do you do with a colleague like that? You make sure that he stays. Easier said than done. As his boss, I wanted to show my appreciation for all his hard work. So, I called his wife and prepared everything. One Friday, just after lunch, I summoned the team to the conference room. In front of everyone, I pulled Micke up and explained that he was greatly appreciated and that we, as a group, wanted to show how happy we were to have him on our team. I said he should take the rest of the afternoon off, take his wife out to dinner, and go to the cinema, and that I would foot the bill. I gave him fifty dollars—you understand that this was some years ago—and two movie tickets. The babysitter was already arranged, so off Micke went. We cheered and applauded a little more, and the whole thing became a big feel-good moment.

Micke didn't say a word. Until afterwards.

He took me aside and gave me one of the worst telling-offs I have ever received. How could I do that to him? Parade him out in front of all twenty-seven people, who just stood and stared at him! Awful! He was just doing his job. He made me promise never to do anything like that again. He was mad with me for a week.

Micke was Green. Does this give you any clues?

Feedback Immunity

There are many ways to give feedback, whether positive or negative, in the wrong way. Now I am going to share some ways you can properly give feedback. The funny thing is that this approach works just as well whether the feedback is positive or negative. Some people are immune to the first kind, others to the latter. I've chosen to focus on negative feedback, as this is typically the most difficult. If you can manage to deliver that, then you can probably manage the positive.

The following advice works just as well for your private life as it does for work. The only thing you need to know is what color your target is. So it begins as usual by you analyzing what colors are in the room. Once you've done that, you just have to set to work. The aim is to get the person to listen to your comments and, ultimately, to create change. All of the challenges of the previous chapter, about how others may perceive the different colors, can be dealt with if you just know how. The next sections explain just that. Many of the basic techniques in each section are similar no matter what color you're talking to, but in each case the way you approach the person will vary depending on who he is and how he'll receive feedback.

How to Give Feedback to a Red—If You Dare

Good news: You don't need any great skill to give negative feedback to a Red. The only thing you need is a Kevlar vest and fire-resistant hair. Because no matter how you do it, the temperature in the room will rise. If you're prepared for it, there won't be any major problems. But if a Red doesn't respond to what you say, then you have reason to worry. Either he's ignoring you and what you're saying or he's seriously ill. But the following scenario is the most common. So hold on to your hat.

Don't Gift Wrap Things

Let me be very clear here—when you're conveying criticism to a Red, the simplest way to do so is to avoid any form of decorative wrapping. It's enough of a challenge to even get through to Reds with your criticism, because a Red always believes that he is right and you are wrong.

Many years ago, I discussed Red behavior with a group of sellers, most of who were Yellow. They understood quite quickly what Red behavior was, and the Reddest person who came to mind at that time was their boss, the sales director. They described him as boorish, a bad listener, completely insensitive, manipulative, unrelenting, often in a foul mood, too much in a hurry, plus a whole bunch of other less flattering descriptors. The group was seriously concerned because they suspected that he hated his staff. Sure, he also worked very hard, and they respected him for that. But since he sometimes asked for ideas and then proceeded to lambast anything that didn't suit his own agenda, they never got anywhere. Besides that, he controlled everything they did, in detail, which was probably the reason he worked so hard. The whole situation sounded disturbing, and the sales team would soon fall apart if nothing was done.

I called the sales director in and explained what the group had said. He listened with increasing interest but without showing any great concern. But his reaction was interesting. Once I had explained to him that his twenty sales reps—the most important resource he had to reach his personal goals—thought that he was an insensitive and aggressive son of a bitch, he replied, "This is just a handful of anecdotes. It's not about me. It's their incompetence that's the problem. If they just worked harder and did a better job, I wouldn't have to push them so hard."

When I explained that his impatience was stressing the group and made the sales reps insecure in their work, he replied that it wasn't his fault. Impatience wasn't a weakness—it was a strength, for Pete's sake! If he were to drag his feet the same way everyone else was doing in this company, nothing would get done. If they just bothered to increase their pace a little bit, then he could calm down and not be so aggressive. But the problem wasn't really him—it was them.

Give Very Concrete Examples

As is often the case with Reds, everyone else was the real cause of the problem. Although Reds are efficient at getting things done, they can also be quick to appoint scapegoats. Remember the competitive element that constantly lies in wait beneath the surface. My way of getting through to this man was to break the whole thing down into tiny pieces and point to specific examples.

For instance, I explained that when he, at nine o'clock on a Friday night, called up a seller to grill him about a particular customer, he ruined the poor man's weekend. There was no point in saying that the sales rep was a nervous wreck or that he couldn't sleep, because this boss would just have ignored it. He wasn't responsible for how people felt. However, I was able to point out that the sales rep would come back to work on Monday morning completely exhausted by the mental effort. And then he wouldn't be able to do his job to the best of his ability. Nothing would be sold that day. By coaching the sales director to give clear answers, I got him to see that he would have problems if his sales team wasn't able to perform. Suddenly he had a reason to rethink.

Stick to the Facts

Another trick to keep in mind: A Red is not that interested in the feelings of others or what people think. He prefers to focus on facts and likes to fix things. He sees himself as an excellent problem solver. I delivered my criticism by placing the boss in the position of the key, the only key to the team's success. Basically, it appealed to his ego. He saw himself as the great leader whose ability to lead the group was the critical factor in creating total dominance in the industry.

Be Prepared for War

So, step by step, example after example, situation to situation, I went through the sales team's perceptions of him. The sales director protested each time and, without exception, argued strongly against any hint of personal criticism. The only thing he did was his job. For every example I gave, I had to repeat the same thing—it didn't matter what he thought; as long as this was what the sales reps thought, he had a problem. He swore and fussed and accused me of incompetence. He would never hire me again. No one would ever hire me again after the uncalled-for attack I had subjected him to. I was finished in the industry.

I refused to play along with his ranting and raving. I leaned back in my chair and waited for the storm to abate. The worst thing you can do in such a situation is play along with the theatrics and start yelling and pounding your fist on the table. The Red's natural instinct to win any given situation will then take over completely. He won't be able to think long term and will become focused on winning right now. He'll ignore the fact that we're working together and that we're going to meet again tomorrow. He's out to win in this moment, even if it costs him a relationship. He ignores the consequences, aggression takes over, and the real battle begins.

But if you refuse to play along, you can manage Reds' anger. So I remained seated, and when he finally calmed down I simply continued to the next point, without saying a single word to indicate that I had been influenced by his ranting and raving. Step by step, I got him to see the impact of his conduct on the group. And little by little, he began to realize that he had to learn to control himself when things didn't go his way at work. He needed to take it easier on other people, to avoid placing unreasonable demands on others, and on himself, and to wait for deadlines instead of demanding delivery a week early, just because he was bored.

Ask the Person to Repeat What You Said

Seen from the outside, this whole incident probably looks like a violent quarrel, but I knew that I could make real progress if I didn't let up. So I did what I recommend everyone trying to give negative feedback to a Red should do—asked the Red to repeat what we'd both just agreed on.

So this sales director had to obediently explain how he would act in the future, point by point, in certain specific situations. (I had a mandate from the CEO to do this, and we both knew it.) And yet even though intellectually he knew that I was right, he couldn't give in. He crossed out one of the less important items on the list, clearly showing that it was a victory for him. Somehow, he still had to win.

Conclusion: Prepare yourself extremely well and try not to give negative feedback to a Red if you are not feeling strong that day. You need to be full of self-confidence, so choose your opportunity carefully. A Red is always strong, always full of self-confidence, so for him it doesn't matter. He will ride into battle at a moment's notice, if necessary. And, prepare yourself for the possibility that he might try to turn the tables. He'll accuse you of everything under the sun so that he can feel he has the upper hand.

Don't fall into his trap.

How to Give Feedback to a Yellow—If You Have the Patience

Yellows are great at many things. Among their great attributes is their love of change. Ideally, they'd change things all the time. You would think that accepting feedback can be a way to start changing the things that need to be improved. In particular, negative feedback is a great way to find out how to raise your performance to a higher level. But this isn't quite the way it works with Yellows.

In fact, that isn't how it works at all. When it comes to change, Yellows are certainly in favor of it, but only if they came up with the idea themselves. Criticism from the outside isn't always well received.

Janne, a good friend of mine, is a phenomenal entertainer. There isn't a group he can't amuse, given enough space. His stories are usually fantastic, and during dinner out they come, a whole succession of jokes so that he has everyone rolling in the aisles. One joke after the other, and the whole thing is extremely entertaining. Janne is truly funny, no doubt about it.

But—and it is a significant but—he dominates everyone else in the room. No one else gets a word in edgeways. If you try, he stops and drowns you out, because he doesn't see you as a partner in a conversation but rather as his audience. After a while, the laughter falls silent and things start to get uneasy. Those of us who know Janne understand that this is due to his desire to constantly demand center stage, while, for others, it takes more time to see through him.

At a dinner party once, it went so far that people started talking about Janne behind his back. I felt bad for him, so I decided to take the bull by the horns.

Make an Agenda—Follow It!

The first thing I had to do was prepare myself. Just sitting down with Janne and speaking from the heart about the issue wasn't going to work. He would just take over the conversation and lure me off the track. So I decided to give a few concrete examples. I also wrote down exactly what effects his behavior might have on people. And I tried to anticipate all his objections.

On one occasion, Janne was helping me in my garden and afterwards we were sitting in the yard, sweaty and exhausted, each of us with a beer in hand. He had just told me about a trip he took to Spain and how frightened he was when the boat that was taking them to the tiny island where they were staying almost capsized. (His wife had already told me that they hadn't even gone by boat. They had taken a small local plane.) But when he stopped for breath, I seized the opportunity.

"Janne," I said. "We need to talk about a serious problem. You talk too much. And you make things up. I know that what you just said isn't true because I spoke to Lena and she said that you flew to the island. This has to stop or you're going to end up on bad terms with people."

Janne stared at me as if I had lost my mind. "I don't talk too much," he said, a little bit surprised. "And even if I did, it would be because I have lots to say. I actually remember a time when I—" I put up a hand in front of his face and moved it quickly back and forth. It silenced him. I went straight on to the next step.

Give Very Concrete Examples

"At the last party we had together, you spoke more than fifty percent of the time we were sitting at the dinner table. I timed you. We were there for two hours and you held court for more than one of them."

"You laughed," he said, now quite grumpy.

"At the beginning. But if you'd been more observant, you would have noticed that it was only at the beginning. And afterwards I heard several people commenting on your need to take center stage in rather a negative way."

This made Janne really indignant. "What ungrateful people! There I was, entertaining people, and what do I get for it? Sheer hostility! A stab in the back!"

"I'm not evaluating what they said," I said, "but I noticed that they thought you were talking too much. Do you understand what I mean?"

It's incredibly important to get the Yellow to acknowledge and accept the message. If you don't recognize a problem, you don't have to solve it. What did Janne do? He nodded morosely. I thought things were going rather well after all.

Then something very strange happened.

Be Aware That His Ears Might Not Be Connected to His Brain

"I understand that you were bored," he said. "You're right. I've told some of those old stories way too many times. I need to stop repeating myself."

I shook my head in despair. He had totally missed the point.

I said, "There's nothing wrong with your stories. You just need to cut down on the number of them. Take every third one. Skip two out of three. The problem is that you talk too much, not that you repeat yourself. You have to let the other seven people around the table speak."

But he wasn't listening; he began telling me a new story just to check if I had heard it before. I had to repeat the whole thing.

Explain That You Don't Dislike Him—Only His Behavior

Criticizing a Yellow is difficult because they take things personally. If everything isn't ice cream and sprinkles all the time, then there must be a problem somewhere. They think you've suddenly become enemies. And Janne reacted in the same way. He physically moved several inches back away from me, a clear signal that he was upset. So I did what you do with little children: I explained that he was still my friend—probably my best friend—and I thought he was really funny. The only thing

I wanted was for him to bury the blabber a little bit. He'd just gone overboard a bit. I told him at least ten times that I liked him very much.

Unfortunately, he's a frightfully bad listener, so I had to remind him of all the fun things we had done together and that I cared tremendously about him. I flattered him and congratulated him on his choice of a new car. I simply manipulated him. A little bit at a time, he began to thaw, and his body language became less defensive.

Prepare Yourself for a Strong Defense Mechanism, Especially the Martyr Complex

But even that wasn't enough. Janne came back with comments like: "Nobody likes me," "Everybody else is much more entertaining," "I thought you thought that I was funny." This was in addition to all the usual defense mechanisms, of course: He was only keeping the party going. It was everyone else who was quiet and boring. What was entertaining about an introverted wallflower? And talking too much— how was that a problem? On the contrary, it was actually a very nice quality. I pointed out that his performances left no room for others to speak or participate.

A concrete example: At the latest dinner, Janne's wife, Lena, was asked a question on five different occasions and every time it was Janne who answered. In the end, it was almost ridiculous. Everyone noticed this except Janne. Lena stopped talking completely.

"But she took so long in answering! And I knew the answer!" He understood nothing. Or he chose to deliberately be slow on the uptake.

Ask the Person to Repeat What You've Agreed To and Follow Up As Soon As You Can

This is easier said than done. Both times we met right after our conversation, he was on the alert. At one point he remained silent during the entire party. Sure, it was a childish way to point out his misery, and it was clearly obvious that he was about to burst with frustration.

Not allowing him to talk was like denying him oxygen. And what irritated him most of all was that no one around the table asked why he wasn't saying anything. Couldn't they see that he was putting on this show for their sake?

What happened was that his wife began speaking more, and people really enjoyed her conversation because she was so pleasant.

After a while, Janne went back to his usual self. It was the easiest way. He saw no direct benefit from keeping quiet. And Lena fell silent again. In Janne's case, I valued our friendship more than trying to change his behavior. I never took up the issue again, but sometimes I take Janne breaks. I simply need to have a good rest from him. If he had been a coworker instead of a friend, I would have followed up several times to ensure he really made a change.

Conclusion: Despite their flexibility and creativity, Yellows are actually the most difficult to change. They don't listen and only implement changes that they themselves have thought of. What you need to do is massage their egos as much as you can bear and put words into their mouths.

It's worth remembering that their short memories also apply to hard feelings. Although they feel awful when criticized, they soon forget. They simply repress everything that is difficult or unpleasant. So if you can just cope with the groans and the moans and maybe a few tears in between, you can continue towards your goal. Achieving that change that will do you both a world of good.

With patience and perseverance, you'll eventually succeed.

How to Give Feedback to a Green—but Think Twice Before You Do

This is the section I would rather skip. Why? you may be wondering. Simple. Criticizing a Green can be cruel. They will feel bad and will simply withdraw and shut down. In general, they have weaker egos and can often be very self-critical. You don't want to increase this burden even more.

It's important to note that there is a difference between being self-critical and changing and being self-critical and not doing anything about it. Many Greens roam through life wishing that things were different. But they rarely have the drive to *do* anything about it. So they continue to be dissatisfied. Sometimes I think that's an end in itself, not to be satisfied. It's a way to get some attention, to gain some power. I know many Greens who control everything and everyone in their families by simply refusing to do anything whatsoever. Psychologists call this being passive-aggressive—a very apt expression.

However, if you would like to give feedback to a Green, here are some methods that might work. Just make sure that you're really committed before you get started.

Give Concrete Examples, and Use a Gentle Approach

Of course, it's always good to be concrete. The difference here is that a Green actually listens, which both previous colors did not. A Green hears what you're saying and dislikes what he hears. But you have to be concrete, and you might be able to do this in the same way as with Reds—but in reverse.

While it doesn't work to tell a Red that you feel bad because of his behavior or that others feel ill at ease because of something he did, that's precisely what works best here. A Green is a relational person and doesn't like to offend. It may seem manipulative, but if a certain form of behavior makes you sad, angry, or just generally dejected say that. A Green person will sense your mood, and he'll pick up what you are saying if you dare to be honest about it.

Be Gentle, but Don't Backpedal

It is all about clarity again. If you have any shred of humanity, you'll see how a Green falls apart the more you give him negative criticism. If you say to your partner that his constant habit of sitting in front of the television watching sports such as football makes you feel completely neglected and unloved, you'll immediately see how much this news affects him. But then it's important that you not backtrack on your statement and say things like "Maybe it's not that bad," or "I still have some projects I've been wanting to work on while you relax." Dare to be clear, and go straight to the point.

You need to convey your message in the right way. Clearly but softly. A hand on someone's shoulder can be enough to send a signal that "we're still friends, but I have a problem when you do this or that."

Deal with the Green's Response "You're Right—I'm So Stupid!"

Total appeasement. A Green's reaction when you tell him how you feel about his behavior is a variation on the Yellow's martyr complex. A Green will prostrate himself, accusing himself of being all kinds of stupid things. Often there will be comments like "I will *never* do that again." Severe compliancy is sometimes unavoidable, and tears may flow. Greens crush themselves with additional arguments about why they're useless and stupid. They'll kneel in your presence for weeks afterwards and try to placate you in all kinds of ways that have nothing to do with the issue at hand.

I heard a story about a man who was told by his wife that she really hated that every single evening he simply had to spend a certain amount of time playing video games (a creature of habit). He admitted that it was childish, unnecessary, and costly. (He spent a considerable amount of money buying upgrades and features for the games.) He promised to be more attentive to her needs. He promised everything and more besides to make up for his dismal behavior. The following six months, he hurried home from work to do the cooking before she arrived. He bought her flowers once a week, and he massaged her feet without her even having to ask.

Very sweet and very appreciated—except that he didn't actually do what she asked him to, namely, to stop playing computer games. He had avoided accepting that particular detail. After all, he had never promised to stop straightaway.

Be Sure to Explain That the Behavior Is the Problem, Not the Person

As with Yellows, dealing with a Green is like dealing with young children—"Daddy loves you, sweetie, but can you please stop eating ice cream on the sofa?" The risk is that the negative feedback will damage your relationship with the person. But you can easily solve this by quickly coming back to the person with good news and positive feedback. In this case, it's not enough just to say that you're only concerned about one problematic issue. You need to show in action that you're not planning to assassinate him. He must be reassured by what you do, not just by what you say.

Ask the Person to Repeat What You Have Agreed On—and Follow Up!

I've noticed that Greens don't always write down what you say to them, so it's a good idea to check with them to make sure you've both interpreted the conversation the same way. If you have a colleague and would like him to be a bit more punctual, make sure he understands that the only issue is his timekeeping. He may very well have gotten the idea that you were actually upset about something else entirely.

We often assume others will behave the same way we would in any given situation. And because Greens can be quite vague when they speak to others and often avoid talking about the real problem, they frequently get the idea that you're really talking about something else. They never go straight to the point themselves, so they assume you haven't, either. So what could you possibly be so unhappy about?

Make sure you're both in agreement about what the problem is. And follow up. We're talking about changing something and creating a new pattern of behavior. And, as usual, Greens will try to solve the problem by doing . . . nothing.

Make sure that doesn't happen!

Conclusion: If you're human, which I think you are, you may have a guilty conscience and think that you went at the Green guy way too hard. I remember one occasion when I argued with an employee because, in my opinion, she didn't do what she was supposed to. Her reaction was to completely fall apart, and she didn't come to work for two days. When we spoke about it afterwards, it turned out that I hadn't actually asked her to do those specific tasks. I'd just assumed that she looked at things the way I did.

I can admit that at the time I was an inexperienced and ineffective boss. I made a classic mistake—I looked at the situation through my own glasses and became furious when her glasses showed something else. And when I realized this later on, I felt quite ashamed of myself. She looked so distressed and went out of her way to avoid meeting me. For a long time I barely dared to say much more than hello and good-bye to her. She did what Greens are good at: She ducked down and did even less work than usual.

Many Greens have an uncanny sixth sense that tells them when it's time to take things extra easy. But here it derailed. This woman did virtually nothing at all because she could sense my guilt and hesitation. She simply took advantage of my bad conscience to get away with it. I lost her completely. In the end, she was laid off because she didn't do her job and I was severely criticized by my boss because I hadn't dealt with the issue.

Make sure that you don't make the same mistake I did. Don't let things go too far. Address the problem while there's still time. So stand up and deliver the negative feedback—even to the friendly Greens in your life.

How to Give Feedback to a Blue—but First, Just a Word of Warning

Before you try to give negative feedback to a Blue, for Pete's sake, make sure you know what you're talking about. Let me remind you that a Blue knows exactly what he's done and he has a far better eye for details than you do. So make sure you have your facts ready before the thought even enters your mind. The section that follows deals with how to deliver feedback, but the biggest task here consists in finding out the details of what happened before you give any feedback.

It may be a good idea to check things out with several other people who are involved in the issue and to document what they say and the facts they offer. The Blue will be able to quote everything and everyone, and he'll always have proof that what he did was correct—after all, that's why he did it. If it had been wrong, he wouldn't have done it. Make sure you're armed to the teeth before scheduling the meeting.

Provide Specific, Detailed Examples, Preferably in Writing

It's not good enough coming in with sweeping phrases like "I think you're working too slowly; can you please speed up?" That's way too general. It doesn't matter if you're right or not—the phrase "working too slowly" says virtually nothing. Says who? Slowly in relation to what?

What you need to do is point to specific accurate and detailed examples. You need to say things like "The latest project took sixteen and a half hours too long." Then add up the effects this has had: "We can't charge the customer for those sixteen and a half hours, which means that profitability has now fallen by $4,125 (16.5 × $250 per hour, or whatever you charge).

This is a message that a Blue might take into consideration. If you were to present it this way to a Yellow it would never work, but for a

Blue this is an extremely relevant piece of information. Because it requires detailed feedback, it would be risky if you were just to present it in a conversation. You need to have everything written down. Blues have a certain degree of distrust when it comes to people talking too much; the written word automatically becomes more true in their eyes.

So write down what you want to say, but double-check everything. And why not actually ask someone else to check the numbers before booking your meeting with the Blue slow coach?

Do Not Get Too Personal If You Don't Know Each Other That Well

A Yellow and a Green boss could easily pat a Blue on the shoulder and be personal in the run-up to a meeting where they are planning to give some tough negative feedback. The reason is simple—they know that they would react very negatively themselves if someone were just to jump straight into criticism without softening them up first. This is the worst way to approach a Blue. He'll just get suspicious and won't listen the way you want him to.

Think about how a Red would have done things. He would simply have booked a meeting, sat down, and shoved the paper with the negative result at the person. (If he had such a paper. If it was about giving feedback to a neighbor about all the leaves that have blown into his garden, he would simply hand him a garbage bag with all the leaves and ask him to count them.) A Red won't dress things up. He gets straight to the point. Usually, he won't have any problem telling you that your work isn't good enough. Having a project drag on is inexcusable, and because he hoped that everything would be finished a day earlier and not a day too late he's now deeply upset.

Stick to the Facts

If you want to get through to a Blue, you need to stick to concrete facts. Each time you start feeling guilty about saying negative things and start speaking about how appreciated he is, you'll confuse him. He'll wonder what you're really trying to say. He has no ego that must be inflated, and he will see right through your attempts to sugar coat the criticism you really have. So stick to the facts.

Don't try the famous sandwich method, used quite extensively by many managers and leaders. In order to defuse and soften a grave message ("you've lost too many customers," "you've cost us money," "you've been rude to Ben in Reception"), you should also say positive things ("you're a valued employee," "you usually do the right thing," "I like you very much") before and after the piece of criticism.

The problem with the sandwich method, commonly known as "praise and blame," is that no one understands your message. What did you really want to say? For a Blue, this will be particularly incomprehensible, because the positive feedback you wrapped your message up in was relational and perhaps emotional—not professional. Remember that he's not there to be your pal, he's there to do a job. Be sure to talk about that.

Feel free to ask if he has any suggestions for improvement. Use words like "quality," "evaluate," "analyze," "follow up." Simply use the language he is used to. You will get through so much more easily.

Be Prepared for Counterquestions at the Molecular Level

Of course he won't buy what you say straightaway. Surely it's reasonable to give him the chance to ask some questions about what you've said. There's a risk that you'll face a host of counterquestions that will make you feel like you're the one being evaluated.

"How do you know?" "Who said that?" "How have you calculated this?" "Where does it say that it must be done that way?" "Why can't I find this information on our intranet?" "Why did you wait until now to give me this feedback?" "Can I have a look at the supporting documents?" "Where's the contract that regulates our billing?" "Are you sure we can't add sixteen and a half hours to this bill?" "Hasn't this been done before? I recall a customer four years ago who . . ."

You might not be able to answer all his questions, so you must simply decide how deep you want to go. You can always say, "That's just the way it is; go back to work now." But this is the worst thing you can do, at least if you want to keep his confidence. The only thing you've proven is that you haven't kept track of the details.

Ask the Person to Repeat What You've Said—and Follow Up Soon Afterwards

When I hold seminars on leadership, the issue of giving feedback is often raised. It's an extremely complicated subject, because we allow our emotions to direct us when we give feedback (and receive it!). But for Blues I give the same advice as I do for other colors: Ask your Blue employee to repeat what you've agreed to. He needs to duly acknowledge that he has seen and heard the same things you have said.

It's very likely that he'll be able to repeat everything more or less verbatim, but it's just as likely that he hasn't taken the message to heart if you were vague in your delivery or too fixed on protecting your relationship. He understands that he should repeat what he knows you want to hear him say. But this isn't the same thing as him believing your negative feedback was relevant.

The example I gave of the overdue project is a treacherous hidden trap. Because a project that's delivered to a customer only has the value the customer believes it to have. Quality is of the utmost importance. If we're careless—according to a Blue's standards—we won't get more orders from that customer. What will the lost revenue cost? So how can you value punctuality as being of more importance than the product itself? At the logical level, a Blue can make your objections seem nonsensical.

But if you know that you're right (not just that it feels right), follow up afterwards to make sure that he's back on track.

Conclusion: It's difficult to criticize a perfectionist. He already knows the best method, and he won't change his opinion just because you happen to have a fancier title on your business card. So it's all about doing your homework very well.

You also need to remember that although it may be difficult to get a Blue to respond to feedback, he has no problem criticizing others. Remember, he sees all the mistakes everyone else makes and he will likely point out your mistakes when you least expect it. Not because he's being vindictive, but just because you've botched up.

14

Who Gets Along and Why It Works

Group Dynamics at Their Finest

The short answer is that a group should consist of all colors to create the best possible dynamic. In a perfect world, we would have an equal number of each color. The Yellow comes up with a new idea, the Red makes the decision, the Green has to do all the work, and the Blue evaluates and makes sure that the results are excellent. But this isn't the case. Not infrequently, we find Yellows in positions better suited to Reds. Or, in the worst cases, they have been able to talk their way into a job that actually requires Blue behavior. Indeed, there are many examples of people who are sitting in the wrong chairs, and part of the explanation lies in the fact that they lack the natural prerequisites to manage their jobs. Moreover, all this has to do with what driving forces different people have. Different people are motivated by different things, and it can cause them to move away from their core behavior in specific situations. But that's a whole other topic and not something I cover in this book.

So how do you put your team together? Look at the picture on the following page. Here you can see why certain combinations are more

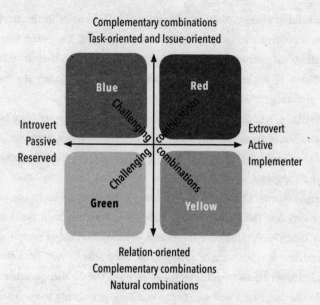

Complementary combinations
Task-oriented and Issue-oriented

Blue   Red

Introvert   Extrovert
Passive   Active
Reserved   Implementer

Challenging combinations

Green   Yellow

Relation-oriented
Complementary combinations
Natural combinations

suitable than others. If you're recruiting members to your team, this may be a good place to start.

As you can see, different colors work differently together. Again, there are plenty of exceptions, but if no one in the group has any knowledge of their behavior pattern some colors will naturally work well together. For instance, it's generally easier for two people to work together if they have the same sense of tempo and work at a similar speed.

Natural Combinations

If we look at the diagram above, we can see that Blue and Green could be a suitable combination, without much of an effort from either of them. They would certainly recognize themselves in each other's ability to breathe calmly and to think twice before doing something. Since both are introverts, each of them feels secure with the other. It's the same kind of energy. Neither of them will build castles in the air, because they prefer to keep both feet on the ground. They don't stress but allow themselves to dive deeply into things. Sure, they may find it difficult to make decisions, but the decisions that they do make will probably be well thought out.

Similarly, Red and Yellow work smoothly together, since they both want to shoot from the hip and always move forward. Here we also have the same kind of energy, only a different type. Both are powerful and outgoing, and because both are verbal, they can easily find the right words. Certainly, they'll have a different focus in the conversation, but the dialogue will still flow. Both set high goals and think quickly. A team of Yellows and Reds will set a fast tempo, and while they are both clear about what they want, they'll motivate those around them to achieve great things. The challenge probably lies in the fact that a Red can perceive a Yellow as being too talkative, but since neither of them is a world-class listener, they'll both just switch off when it suits them.

Complementary Combinations

It also works to look at the other axis and make pairings based on each color's focus. Both Blues and Reds are task oriented. Reds are certainly more interested in the result than in the process itself, and Blues are more concerned with the process and tend to ignore the result—but they're at least speaking the same language. Both devote themselves to work and only spend limited time chatting about football or home improvement—except maybe at lunchtime. They would complement each other in a good way. If we liken this to a car, a Red is the accelerator, while a Blue is the brake. Both are needed in order to drive successfully. The trick is not to push both pedals at the same time.

Similarly, there is some logic in placing a Green with a Yellow.

The tempo at which they work will be different, but both of them will be curious about each other. Both believe that people are interesting and important. While one likes to take it easy, the other likes having fun. They'll easily find a similar focus. The Green will allow the Yellow to take as much space as he wants. One talks; the other listens. It can work out well. In addition, Greens are good at calming down the slightly hysterical Yellows, who sometimes have a hard time staying grounded. Of course, there's a risk that they'll fail to devote sufficient time to the work itself, but they will have a very good time. People around them might feel that they're *only* having a good time and not actually delivering anything. As both can find it difficult to say no, it might also be a good idea to avoid entrusting them with too much money.

Challenging Combinations

At the same time, there are two very complicated combinations. This doesn't mean that they won't be able to work together, but it definitely means that there are obstacles that need to be considered. One possible solution is that both of them become more self-aware in the ways that they work and interact with each other.

Look at the illustration on the following page.

The right column shows the things the person himself sees in his profile. The left column shows how his exact opposite could perceive him in less favorable circumstances. You've probably heard that a person is a real bore, only to meet him and discover a very interesting person with lots of exciting things to say. Who's right and who's wrong? It depends on whom you ask.

The problem lies in the interaction between each color and its exact opposite. The positive image expresses how each profile experiences himself. The negative image is an expression of how he can be experienced by others. We all see different things.

BLUE: ANALYTICAL		RED: DOMINANT	
NEGATIVE	POSITIVE	NEGATIVE	POSITIVE
Critical	Diligent	Pushy	Strong-willed
Indecisive	Thoughtful	Strict	Independent
Narrow-minded	Serious/Persistent	Tough	Ambitious
Fastidious	Demanding	Dominant	Determined
Moralizing	Methodical	Hard	Effective

GREEN: STABLE		YELLOW: INSPIRING	
NEGATIVE	POSITIVE	NEGATIVE	POSITIVE
Stubborn	Supportive	Manipulative	Inspiring
Uncertain	Respectful	Hot-tempered	Stimulating
Compliant	Obliging	Undisciplined	Enthusiastic
Dependent	Reliable	Counteractive	Dramatic
Awkward	Pleasant	Egotistic	Outgoing

Genuine Problems

It would be quite a challenge to put a Red and a Green together issues solve a problem. If the task depends on effective cooperation, then issues will quickly arise. In the beginning, the Green is very passive, especially when compared to the Red, who gets going even before he's heard the instructions. While the Greens think it's burdensome to have to do their part, the Reds have already started in a hurry.

The Red will be very critical of the Green's constant moaning about the amount of work. At the same time, the Green will think that the Red is an aggressive son of a bitch who never listens. Nevertheless, under favorable circumstances it may work out. In general, a Green is prepared to cooperate; that's their strength. They function well with many other people because they're more accommodating than demanding. So there can be a certain logic in setting a Red with a Green. A Red likes giving orders, and a Green is usually okay with receiving orders.

Based on Marston's theories (see page 227), the greatest challenge of all is to ask a Yellow and a Blue to work together. If neither of them is aware of how their personalities work, there will be friction from the outset. The Yellow dives into the task without the slightest idea what to do or how to do it. He doesn't read any instructions, and he doesn't listen long enough to find out what the task is actually about. He'll speak at great length about what an exciting project they've been given. In the meantime, the Blue starts reading and researching all the material available. He doesn't say a word but just sits there. More or less motionless—he thinks.

The Yellow, on the one hand, will consider him to be the most un-inspiring bore he has ever met. The Blue, on the other hand, will only be disturbed by the Yellow's perpetual verbal barrage. He'll slowly begin to boil beneath the surface because of the incessant buzzing around him. He believes that the Yellow is a frivolous windbag, not deserving any attention whatsoever. And when the Yellow finally re-alizes that he hasn't won the Blue over to his side, he'll pull out all the stops and talk even more. In the worst case, he'll try to charm the Blue, which will end up driving them to disaster. They'll sit in their own corners, with faces like they've tasted sour milk, both mad for completely different reasons.

Self-awareness, my friend, is the solution.

Go Green!

It is not easy to read and interpret everyone. If a person only has one color, then you won't have any problems with him once you've finished reading this book. It will be obvious what you should do. A person who is only Red or only Yellow is hard to miss. But even the genuine Greens or Blues are quite easy to detect if you know what to look for.

As I mentioned earlier, statistically speaking only about 5 percent of the population has just one color that shows in their behavior. Around 80 percent have two, and the rest have three. No one has four, not with the tool that I use.

It's also relatively easy to recognize people who have two colors. Two color combinations normally follow any of the axes. So they are: Blue/Red, Red/Yellow, Yellow/Green, or Green/Blue.

It does happen, of course, that purely opposite qualities can be found in one and the same person. I've met lots of Yellow/Blue people. There is nothing wrong with that; it's just less common. But what's really unusual is distinctly Red/Green profiles. Why this is the case I don't know.

On one occasion, I met a woman who was a middle manager working for a company in the car industry. She was determined and powerful in her manner, but, at the same time, she was extremely caring. Her care and attention for her employees was genuine, and it had some strange results. Among other things, she could lose her temper very quickly. Her telling-offs were legendary. Once she realized this, however, she would do whatever she needed to soften the effects of her actions and repair the damage. She felt genuinely bad for having been hard on various individuals, but at the same time she couldn't control herself. This friction between the two conflicting colors in her behavior (Red and Green) meant that she was very close to burnout.

People with three colors will always be more difficult to interpret. If someone is very difficult to place on the map, it may very well be because he has three colors. The situation will determine what his behavior will be.

The best advice I can give if you really can't analyze the person you meet is to shut your mouth and start listening. Simply act Green if you are unsure. People sometimes tells me that they can't understand a certain person because he doesn't do anything. But even a person who is very passive exhibits some form of behavior. And at this stage, you know what color is associated with someone who doesn't do much—that's a common Blue behavior.

15

Written Communication

How to Evaluate Someone When You Can't Meet in Person

Many things are revealed in the way we write. Different colors have distinct writing styles; some take the time to express themselves, while others keep brief. If you have the chance to read through a longer writing sample that the person in question has written—a report, a column, a letter, or a letter to the editor—you have lots to go on. Very often it's possible to detect a color in the written word. If you're a person of few words in speech, you can also be the same in your writing. And vice versa.

If the only thing you have is an email, then you have to go on what you have. Let's say that you're replying to a customer's message. You want to prepare yourself properly. You look carefully at how his email reads. Is it factual? Is there any kind of personal touch? Is it short and concise, or does it seem to have been written a little spontaneously? All of these little details are important signals that you can use to your advantage. As usual, there are plenty of exceptions, but there are still patterns to be aware of.

Here are some examples of what this can look like.

From: kristian.jonsson@teamcommunication.com
To: Cina.cinasson@coco.net
Subject: Meeting
Meeting tomorrow morning at 11. BE PUNCTUAL!
-K

What do you think? Is K screaming because he used capital letters? It's not clear. It could be that he just wanted to stress that the time for the meeting is important. Maybe he was rushing out somewhere. It doesn't matter to him that the person receiving the email might be put off by the abrupt style and the caps lock. As always, a Red can live with that. Get a grip! He just wanted to be clear.

Your action: Reply instantly! Be short and concise. One way might be to simply reply: "Okay."

From: kristian.jonsson@teamcommunication.com
To: Cina.cinasson@coco.net
Subject: Meeting
Hello, Cina! What's up? Were you at the game last night? I saw that Lasse was there. He spilled his drink all over himself, and I thought that I would never stop laughing! Check out the picture I put on Facebook. By the way, I thought that we could sit down and chat about that customer tomorrow morning before lunch if it works for you. Is eleven o'clock okay?
Ciao! Krille

From: kristian.jonsson@teamcommunication.com
To: Cina.cinasson@coco.net
Subject: Meeting
Oh, I forgot to attach the photo. Anyway, here it is.
Krille

Even in writing, a Yellow expresses himself in a very spontaneous and easygoing manner. He likes to share stories and keep things personal. Note the social babble about poor Lasse and his drink. A good laugh that must be highlighted to attract your attention.

Your reply? There isn't any need to rush, but don't fail to respond or he'll feel insecure. Be cordial as well. Don't forget to thank him for the funny picture and mention that you laughed at his story. . .

> From: kristian.jonsson@teamcommunication.com
> To: Cina.cinasson@coco.net
> Subject: Meeting
> I just wanted to remind you about the meeting tomorrow at eleven. Hope it still works for you. I'm going to bring in some homemade cinnamon buns to have with our coffee. Have a good one!
> With kind regards, Kristian

A softer, more personal tone. Kristian had probably polished this email appropriately, to make sure there was nothing controversial in it. Reminding people about meetings that were booked a long time previously can be perceived as slightly offensive by some people, so here we want to be certain that nothing can be misinterpreted.

And how do you respond to this pleasant email? Be personal and benign in return. Express your thanks. You don't have to say that it will be great to have some cinnamon buns, but if you do it won't do any harm. Then remember to take it easy and not to stress at the meeting.

> From: kristian.jonsson@teamcommunication.com
> To: Cina.cinasson@coco.net
> Subject: Meeting
> Good morning, Christina.

Ahead of tomorrow's meeting with our client, I would appreciate it if you could familiarize yourself with the necessary background information.

I've attached three documents relating to the issue.

Greetings,

Kristian Jonsson

 + 46704808080

Copy of dates and participants.xls

IT Strategy Update UGMT.doc

Flyer Template 27 Nov 2014.doc

The original invitation to the meeting was sent out a long time ago, but you've already figured that out, right? An alarm was probably set on the computer to send out a reminder about the meeting a day beforehand. The text in the email is factual and doesn't contain even a trace of a personal touch. There is a little note reminding you that it's best to be well prepared.

What's the best way to answer this Blue email? Confirm that you've received it along with the files. Say that you will get back to him if you have any questions after reading through the material. And know that the sender assumes you'll read the whole thing carefully.

16

What Makes Us as Mad as Hell?

Temperament Can Reveal Everything About a Person

At the end of this book, I will present you with a history lesson. It is all about Hippocrates' four temperaments, describing the same differences that this book is all about.

It's possible to draw conclusions about someone's behavior based on his temperament. By "temper" or "temperament" I don't just mean what frustrates a person but rather how he reacts when something unexpected happens. Another way of saying this might be to talk about a person's disposition. It can be how he reacts to changing circumstances and what sort of energy he has.

But yes, anger is a good and exciting gauge by which to judge a person's color. Moreover, it's situational. What upsets one person may not upset someone else in the least. By observing how someone reacts when things go wrong, you can get some important clues. Let me give you an example of a quick diagnosis.

What the hell . . . ! ! !

For the sake of simplicity, let's compare different temperaments to different types of drinking glasses. I would suggest a shot glass for a

Red temperament. "But," you might say, "that little glass doesn't hold much."

Indeed it doesn't, and many Reds function like that, too. It doesn't take much for them to lose their temper and erupt. It could be about traffic jams, missed phone calls, someone moving too slowly on the escalator. Not getting their own way. That someone is just generally dense. Remember that of all the colors they are the ones most often surrounded by idiots. For a Red, there are many reasons to be irritated. A Red's strength is that when they explode they rid themselves of any anger or irritation they've been feeling. They erupt briefly, but it doesn't last. The shot glass may be quick to reach capacity, but it doesn't take long to empty it. They simply empty the shot glass of anger and frustration and they're back to being themselves. (I'm not referring to how those around a Red perceive things.)

The advantage is that, for all their raging, it usually subsides quite quickly. A Red can rarely manage to be angry for long. He blurts out what he wants to say, and then he moves on. Sure, he can leave many confused people around him, but that's their problem. He's finished with the episode. Then something deeply upsetting happens again, and he just erupts. And again. And again.

Imagine that you pick up the shot glass and pour it out over your desk. Not nice, but quite manageable. You can always clean it up.

But remember the shot glass fills up just as quickly as it was emptied. It will happen again. Many perceive a Red's temperament as totally unpredictable. It can erupt at any time.

Nevertheless, I don't think it's that unpredictable. If you know the person in question, you probably also know what triggers his anger.

However, it's important to know that a Red doesn't consider himself an angry person. He's just given someone a piece of his mind or maybe raised his voice at him. Again, it's just a way of communicating. But to a Green, it might seem that a Red is angry even when he's just sharing his opinion. So much is in the eye of the beholder. It's common that many people simply back off, to avoid confronting the Red and triggering his anger. But by letting their anger get the best of them all the time, Reds miss out on a lot of feedback.

"I Am Very Upset! Do You Even Hear What I'm Saying?"

Even the cheerful Yellow loses his temper: Don't let anyone tell you otherwise. Although Yellows generally have a sunny, optimistic disposition, they have a temper as well. Like Reds, they are active, perceptive people. This means that they have a lot to react to. And if you're quick-thinking and your tongue sometimes gets away from you, well then, things can happen. What comes out your face's front door isn't always well thought out.

Because Yellows are very expressive and emotional at the same time, you'll know in advance when the mercury starts rising. An observant person won't have any problem noticing that a Yellow is on the verge of bursting. The look in his eyes intensifies; his gestures become impetuous; his voice is raised. All this happens, but it happens gradually.

If the Red temperament is like a shot glass, then we can liken the Yellow temperament to an everyday drinking glass. It holds more and it's easier to see when it's full. The level rises a little at a time, and if you're paying attention you'll have no problem observing this as it happens.

Now, if we take the tumbler of milk and pour it out all over your desk what's the result? It will be a lot messier and much soggier than when we poured out the shot glass, right? Many important papers are destroyed, and it requires more than a single paper towel to dry it all up.

But we can still handle the situation. Even this temperamental outburst can be managed without too many serious complications.

There are also advantages in a Yellow's temperament. He'll feel guilty that he laid into someone close to him: colleague, family member, neighbor, or maybe even you. So he'll make an extra effort to be kind the next time you meet. He'll have an uneasy conscience, something a Red wouldn't be able to comprehend.

If a person happens to be a combination of Red and Yellow, things can get tough. In this case, there's a lot of ego in the room, and you won't quite know what's happening.

Depending on the driving forces and motivational factors the individual may have, he can assert his own position almost to the point of absurdity. Genuine Yellows can let their egos get in the way most of the time. The advantage, however, is that due to their bad memory, they don't hold grudges for long. They quickly forget that there were any problems, an ability that can make Greens and Blues find Yellows to be a little bit too exciting.

Beware the Fury of a Patient Man. Beware Indeed.

Do you recognize this old saying? The person who coined it probably had a Green in mind. You may never have seen a Green lose his temper. It may very well be that your good friend, the friendly and gentle pal you've never had a serious argument with, hasn't ever shown even a shred of bad temper.

Does that mean that this is a person who can't get angry? Not at all. It just means that instead of turning his temper outwards, it's oriented in another direction. Inwards.

I would liken a Green's temperament to a fifty-gallon beer barrel. Can you imagine how many shot glasses it would take to fill it? We could fill, fill, and fill even more before we even start covering the bottom of it. Many Greens function like that. They receive and accept without objecting. This is very much connected to their desire to avoid conflict but also to their inability to say no. They simply agree because it's easier that way.

Does this mean that Greens don't have their own opinions? Not at all; they have just as many opinions about things as anyone else. They just don't talk about their opinions. And this is often the problem. They fill the barrel. Week in and week out, a Green accepts one perceived injustice after the other—note that I said "perceived." It may take several years before the barrel is full.

Now take this barrel, lift it up, and pour the contents out over your desk.

What happens? Everything will be washed away. The water in the barrel will not only wash away everything on your desk away; even the desk itself and you along with it will go out with the flood, too. There's no stopping it.

"You said that I didn't finish the project on time? Really? Really?! Last week, you said that I didn't do it well enough. Now let me tell you this: A year ago you promised me a new office, and it still hasn't materialized. And when I was hired here, back in 1997, you said the same thing, and now let me tell you . . ."

Everything has to come out. Just make sure that you're not the spark that sets it all off.

The problem is large-scale. Greens don't release any anger or frustration but control their emotions so as not to create trouble or stand out. But they feel and experience just as much as everyone else does. They just lack the natural tools to release everything. But we can help by becoming facilitators. We can ask questions, invite them in, and look for signals. Look at their body language to see if there are signs of disapproval. Create a healthy environment around a Green so that he becomes comfortable enough to say what he thinks so that he doesn't have to continually compromise his position. Otherwise, he will turn all his frustration inwards. And we know what this kind of stress can do to a person.

I have my own private theory, which I certainly cannot prove scientifically, but I suspect that this may be the main reason why Greens suffer burnout. They carry anxiety, anguish, and even anger for so long that it eventually makes them ill. It's a noticeable problem that should be taken seriously.

A Complaint a Day

During an extremely stressful period in my earlier career in the banking sector, I once heard a comment about a Blue. All of us were working every day and night, and many of us were showing the stress. Frustration was hanging in the air.

Our credit controller was in the middle of the whole thing. Nothing got to her. She never even acted stressed. Her face was absolutely indecipherable, and her gestures were as limited and moderate as always. While the rest of us ate our lunch on the go, she took her full sixty minutes and ate in peace and quiet . . . it was as if nothing could disturb her peace.

Then one of my Yellow-Red colleagues said, "She's not normal. She doesn't have any feelings in her body."

Back then, it sounded logical to me, but when you think about it, it can't be true. Blues simply have less need to communicate than Greens. So they simply don't do it. Some things are turned inwards even for Blues. Those who are quick thinkers may wonder if Blues run the risk of burnout just as much as Greens do. Not at all. They have a system to keep stress under control.

Metaphorically speaking, Blues have as big a beer barrel as Greens have, but there is one crucial difference: At the bottom of the barrel, there's a handy little tap. This tap gives a Blue a valve to release part of the contents of the barrel. He can regulate the pressure whenever he wishes to.

Moreover, the tap leaks. It's not tight enough to create a perfect seal, and small drops drip most of the time. A Blue's dissatisfaction comes out in the form of tiny grumblings.

"Just look. Someone has misplaced the pen again! Typical! Now I'll have to finish this off myself. As usual, I get the most boring task. There's no structure here. Typical."

And so he goes on. His pinpricks affect those around him, but what they hear all the time is just a muttering trumpet. The embers don't fan into a fire. We interpret it as a perpetual whining, but the discontent is real. And because a Blue isn't sufficiently active to instigate something, he'll argue about things rather than doing something about them. It's all based on complaints that others should see what he sees, that he doesn't have any authority to act, or that he's simply in a bad mood. But for him, this is a great way of keeping the pressure under control. So the barrel will never need to be emptied out over somebody's desk, and thus serious catastrophes are avoided.

The way to manage his nagging is to ask counterquestions. Ask for concrete examples. Ask for suggestions for improvement. It may, in fact, be the case that the Blue has solved the problem that is plaguing him, but that he needs a straight question in order for him to step forward and suggest a solution.

What Can You Do About the Fact That People Don't Get Pissed Off in the Same Way?

With these simple observations in mind, you can quickly form an idea of what type of person you're dealing with. Pay attention to how he reacts under stress and pressure.

But, at the same time, remember that no system is perfect. These are only indications, and they apply only to individual colors. Besides, as I wrote previously, different situations can give rise to completely different forms of conduct. Generally speaking, the more important a particular thing is for a certain person, the stronger his reaction will be.

See for yourself. If someone insults your neighbor, you might think it was unfair. But you don't make a big scene out of it. However, if someone were to insult your husband or wife, you would be absolutely furious. That's just one example. There are many levels and degrees of difference to reflect on.

17

Stress Factors and Energy Thieves

What Is Stress?

Anger is one thing. Stress is another. Sometimes one is a consequence of the other, but not always. Some people become angry because of stress; others become stressed because of anger. When we speak about stress, we often mean the feeling of having too much to do and too little time to do it. There's not enough time to do everything at work and then on top of that factor in the time needed to go to the gym, meet with friends, spend time with family, do various kinds of recreational activities, oh, and maybe sleep.

However, the stress that makes us truly suffer is often due to things apart from a lack of time. If you feel pressure and have high expectations about what you will do and how you are meant to be, you can become stressed, even if you aren't really pressed for time.

Pressure, demands, and expectations create stress and can make you feel self-critical and powerless. You may find it difficult to sleep or may feel physical pain in your body. Simply put, the feeling of stress arises when we experience greater demands and expectations than we can cope with.

Different People React Differently to Stress: What a Surprise!

Seriously, though, all of us react differently to stress. Different people can experience the same event in different ways, and a person can experience similar events differently at different times. The things you have been through in the past and how you are feeling right now all have an effect on how you act and react.

If you're well rested and feeling fine, you could experience a tough week at work as an invigorating challenge, despite your heavy workload. But if you're tired and feeling down on yourself, you may experience the same week as something horrible and demoralizing.

How does your color affect your stress? It says nothing about your stress threshold (that is, how much stress you can bear). But it can say something about *what* stresses you and how you'll react to stress. Previously, I mentioned the concept of driving forces—whatever forces motivate me to get up out of bed every morning, dash to work, and go the extra mile. This book doesn't deal with this dimension, but it's easy to see that we become stressed when we feel that we're spending too much time on the wrong things.

Once you've understood what the most important stress factors in your life are, you'll be better equipped to avoid them when possible. If you're a manager responsible for a number of people and you know their behavior profiles, you can avoid the worst pitfalls. A great deal of stress can be avoided if you know how. And you can retain the group's productivity.

The rest of the chapter is written with an element of irony, and I urge you to read it in that way.

Stress Factors for Reds

If you would like to stress out a Red, you can try one of the following to lower his self-confidence.

Take Every Form of Authority Away

Not being involved in decision-making is really difficult for a Red. He always believes that he has better ideas and so he also believes that he should be the one in charge of the project.

Achieve No Results Whatsoever

"If we're not making immediate headway, then all our work has been a waste." Such an insight can trigger severe stress reactions in a Red, and those around him should be on their guard. He'll look for scapegoats.

Eliminate Any Kind of Challenge

If everything is too easy, it becomes boring. Red behavior hinges on one thing: the ability to handle problems and difficult challenges. If there are no problems to solve, then Reds will lack stimulation. They'll become passive, believing that they have absolutely nothing to do. They can slow down the pace, and this can be difficult to reverse.

Waste Time and Resources and Work as Inefficiently as Possible

Just sitting around doing nothing is a waste of time. Not that this is necessarily what we're actually doing, but, in the mind of a Red, if you don't get the maximum productivity out of your time, it's wasteful and particularly stressful from a managerial perspective. He is probably evaluated on the organization's efficiency.

Make Sure That Everything Becomes a Routine

Mundane and repetitive tasks are the kiss of death for a Red. It's simply boring. Reds lose their concentration and will find something else to do. Routine work is not what they're good at. They're lousy at details, and they know it. Someone else needs to take care of the dull, routine work, because a Red believes that he has a better understanding of the big picture.

Make a Bunch of Stupid Mistakes

Mistakes are one thing, but stupid mistakes, well, that's something completely different. It's so overwhelmingly unnecessary. If a Red believes his colleagues are brainless, he gets crazy: "Why don't they understand what they're supposed to do? How hard can it be?"

Give Him No Control over Others

A Red's need for control can be extensive. It's not about controlling facts and details. They want to control people. What they do, how they do it, and so on. Without this control, a Red gets very frustrated.

Tell Him Regularly to Cool Down or to Lower His Voice

They get crazy when people say that they're angry when they're not. They will always be a little more hot-tempered than average, but this doesn't actually mean that they're angry. And it's precisely this accusation that can get them to become angry—really angry.

What Does a Red Do When He Gets Stressed and Feels Pressured?

He blames everyone else. As a Red is often surrounded by idiots, it's easy for him to single out scapegoats. And he can easily overdo things when he wants to take someone to task for having made a mess of things. Be aware! That's my advice to you, because you'll feel the sting of his wrath.

Reds are always more demanding than other colors. They expect a lot from themselves, and they expect a lot from you. When under stress, they're also excessively demanding and driven—much more than usual.

The Red will shut out his other colleagues. He becomes closed, burrows into the task at hand, and works even harder. Remember that his anger and frustration is lurking just beneath the surface, so please be careful about what you do in his presence.

Can I Help Reds to Manage Their Stress?

If you have the authority to give a direct order, the answer is simple: Ask them to get a hold of themselves. It actually works. Another way to make it easier for Reds in stressful situations is to send them home and tell them to do some physical exercise—anything to burn some of that frustrated, restless energy. Send them to a place where they can run in some kind of competition, spending their energy on winning something that will be of no importance to the group. When they come back, most of their aggression will have dissipated.

Stress Factors for Yellows

If for any reason, you would like to get a Yellow to feel stress, try one of the following to get him off balance.

Pretend He's Invisible

You remember a Yellow's driving impulse, right? "Look at me! Here I am!" If you want to get him off balance, simply make him feel invisible. If he's not visible, then he doesn't exist. He feel ignored and over-looked, and this is guaranteed to cause stress.

Become Very Skeptical

Any person manifesting lots of skepticism is very negative, some-thing that stresses Yellows. They want to see the positive and the light and consider even everyday realists to be prophets of doom. Pes-simism and negativity effectively kill Yellows' enthusiasm and cause them to feel tense.

Structure Work as Much as Possible

Just like Reds, Yellows shun routine, repetitive tasks and jam-packed schedules. They happily create schedules for others, but they can't follow them themselves. Force them into one of your plans and you'll see how your Yellow friends will begin to unravel.

Isolate Him from the Rest of the Group

For a Yellow, the absence of someone to talk to is perhaps the worst thing ever. It's the end of the world. Because they need to talk, there must be someone there to listen. Being trapped in an office space with only a desk for company is a punishment worse than death. It's like being deported to Siberia.

Make Clear That It's Inappropriate to Joke at Work

"No joking around and no sense of humor? Is this a funeral par-lor?" I once got exactly that comment from a Yellow who discovered that consultants didn't have time to monkey about. She was very stressed out by all the seriousness and left before her probation period was over.

Push a Yellow to Think Carefully Beforehand—Twice

Suppressing a Yellow's spontaneity is like holding down the lid on a saucepan when the milk is boiling over. It simply doesn't work. It creates a terrible mess, and everyone gets involved when Yellows—loudly and intensely—invite everyone else into their stress spiral. Remember that a Yellow's stress will always be noticed. Don't believe otherwise.

Continuously Squabble and Fuss About Insignificant Things

Having to face incessant confrontations is exhausting. This is something of a paradox, because Yellows aren't afraid of conflict like Greens. But if there's too much bickering, it will disrupt their desire for fun and positivity, which causes stress. They can cope with squabbling, but when it becomes too much, Yellows won't be at the top of their game and they lose their usual luster.

Try a Little Public Humiliation

A Yellow who has been given negative feedback in the presence of others won't be a pleasant sight to behold. It's enough to make him never speak to you again. Moreover, he'll also become incredibly defensive, and you'll achieve nothing at all.

What Does a Yellow Do When He Gets Stressed and Feels Pressured?

Be prepared for the fact that he'll draw attention to himself even more than usual. His ego makes it impossible for him not to seek out more attention and affirmation, since he has to compensate for the negative feelings of stress. This means that he'll actively look for attention, which makes him feel better. The risk is that he'll talk too much and force himself into the center of everything.

Maybe you thought that this wasn't possible, but he also runs the risk of becoming excessively and unrealistically optimistic. You've never experienced a real challenge until you've tried to cope with a truly stressed-out Yellow. He'll come up with plans that are so wild and outlandish that not even he can believe them. This is just a natural coping mechanism for him.

Can I Help Yellows to Manage Their Stress?

Let a Yellow organize a party. He urgently needs to meet people in social contexts. He can sink very deep into his own misery if he remains under stress for too long. When things are at their worst, suggest a pub crawl, a party, or why not just a simple barbeque? It doesn't need to be fancy, but make sure he gets to enjoy himself for a while. Also, make sure that it's *fun*!

Stress Factors for Greens

If you, for any reason, would like to get a Green to feel stress, I propose the following unpleasant things.

Take Every Form of Security Away from Him

Give him tasks that he's never done before without explaining anything whatsoever to him. But, at the same time, expect perfect implementation. Leave him alone in meetings with people who place unreasonable demands on him. Don't support him when things heat up in a conversation. Send an angry Red to rant at him. The stress will soon follow.

Leave Lots of Loose Ends

Unfinished tasks and loose ends are deeply disturbing. Greens like to know how things fit together, and when they don't understand how

the process works it won't go well. Unfinished projects—things that
have been started but are drawn out without any end in sight—really
mess things up for Greens. This is why Yellows are phenomenal at causing stress for Greens.

Hang Around Him Constantly

If a Green doesn't get his private space, if there's nowhere he can
withdraw from the world, he gets very stressed. He likes other people,
of course, but he needs to be alone with himself also. If this isn't possible, then he can't think anymore.

Make Lightning-Fast Changes and Unexpected Changes of Direction

This is the specialty of Reds and Yellows. Quick decisions that they
don't always explain. Greens are miserable when they're forced into
making unexpected and rapid changes, and they often respond by
ending up in a state of absolute indifference. The worst kind of change
is when a Green gets an order in the morning and just as he begins to
reflect on how he will do it a counterorder comes.

Ask Him "Would You Be So Good as to Redo the Whole Thing from Beginning to End?"

Having to redo a task is synonymous with failure. If something
must be redone, it can only be because your work wasn't good enough
the first time. In other words, negative feedback. By extension, this
means that you're not good enough as a person, which, of course, is
extremely stressful.

Tell a Green, "Look Here! We Can't Agree on Absolutely Everything."

Disagreements in a work group or in the family inevitably lead to
stress. Only troublemakers enjoy conflict. Friction in the most impor-

tant group, the family, is particularly serious. A Green won't know what he should do.

Push Him into the Spotlight

Under no circumstances will Greens want to take center stage when they're in larger groups. Groups of more than three people would be considered large groups unless the Green knew everyone very well. If you force a Greens into such a situation, he'll just stare at his feet. Everyone can see how uneasy he is, and the rest of the group will also be stressed. Not good.

What Does a Green Do When He Gets Stressed and Feels Pressured?

He becomes very reserved and almost cold. His body language becomes rigid and closed, and if you're the one who triggered his stress he won't have anything to do with you. Some Greens can exhibit strong apathy. They become cold and unsympathetic even towards people whom, in normal circumstances, they care very much about.

They also become very hesitant and uncertain. Stress makes Greens insecure and afraid of making mistakes. It can be at work but also at home. If a child gets sick, a Green becomes passive and just looks on, because he's afraid of doing the wrong thing. He'll also internalize the blame for the situation and may become completely closed.

At work, it may be slightly different. It depends. Many Greens end up in a rut of obstinacy or stubbornness, provoking those around them by refusing to change anything. Even when they see that a particular method is not working well, they can refuse to act. It seems strange, but the typical Green stubbornness gets the upper hand and prevents them from doing anything.

Can I Help Greens to Manage Their Stress?

Allow them to do nothing. Give them free time for things like gardening, sleep, or other forms of relaxation. Maybe something like sending them off to a movie—not with a large group of people, but possibly on their own—or giving them a good book that takes two days to read. They don't really want to do anything. Let them do nothing until the stress subsides. Then they'll be back to their normal selves.

Stress Factors for Blues

If you, for any reason, would you like to get a Blue to feel stress, just upset every one of his calculations.

Tell Him, "You Don't Know What You're Talking About."

You may think that Blues don't take criticism personally, but if they believe that the criticism is untrue and unfounded, it can be very hard on them. Not because they're afraid of conflict, or that your relationship will suffer, but because their sense of perfection is being besmirched.

Have the Management Team Make a Spontaneous Decision

A Blue is often okay with change, because he doesn't ever consider anything completely perfect. But he needs to know the motivations behind the change. If it's not in the plan, then it's unplanned, and a lack of planning indicates poor structure—not good. Inevitably, this leads to headaches.

Tell Him, "This Could Be Risky or Uncertain, but We're Going to Go Ahead Anyway."

There's a certain amount of risk in everything. A Blue sees risks everywhere. If a Red were to say that jumping from a plane without a parachute is a huge risk, a Blue would say that it's risky to buy a new lawn mower. You never really know what can happen. And the faster things go, the greater the risks become.

Surprise Him with Something like "Your In-laws Are Coming Over Unannounced! Fantastic!"

It's a matter of order and structure, of working at a relaxed pace or renovating the kitchen according to a clearly established plan. If half the family were to drop in all of a sudden, it would upset everything. You should never try to surprise a Blue. Since he may not have communicated his own plans completely, you can create quite a problem.

Say, "Whoopsadaisy, What Happened Here?"

Mistakes are made by blockheads and careless people. Blues don't make mistakes, so when everyone else makes a mess of things and disrupts his plans a Blue might simply close the door and refuse to listen. He doesn't want to hear that the project has crashed; he just wants to keep doing his part—even if that task no longer makes any sense.

Tell Him, "Forget About the Bureaucracy. Let's Innovate!"

"Don't you have any imagination? We have to be a bit more flexible here." This is a great way to get a Blue to lose his footing at work. People who break the rules and go against the regulations are to be regarded with suspicion, and you need to keep them on a short leash. If a Blue realizes that he's in the hands of an organization that pays no attention whatsoever to proper procedures, he can show considerable resistance.

Remind Him, "We Simply Need to Take Bigger Risks."

A variation on the preceding point. Right is right, and proper preparation is the be-all and end-all, the Alpha and Omega. It even says so in a book. So when a Blue can't prepare himself in his (sometimes extremely cumbersome) way, it triggers stress. He's the opposite of spontaneous, and you simply can't force a Blue to respond to a situation before he's had time to acquaint himself with the subject. He'll have so many reservations he won't be any use.

Surround Him with Overly Emotional People

Nope. Sloppy sentimentality is downright unpleasant. It's messy and awkward, and a Blue doesn't like it. Logic is what counts, and if you overlook this, he'll find it very trying. He'll make himself scarce, and he'll never forget that you're an overly emotional person who doesn't use your brain in the same way he uses his.

What Does a Blue Do When He Gets Stressed and Feels Pressure?

He becomes excessively pessimistic. Oh yes. It actually gets worse than usual. Suddenly everything becomes pitch black, and he falls into a pit of despair. Lethargy is common, and nothing is of interest anymore. Gloom and doom will rain down on all of us. He also gets unbearably pedantic. When they feel stress, many people increase their pace in order to compensate. Not a Blue. He stomps on the brakes. Now isn't the time for making any mistakes. Those around him can expect constant criticism. He'll suddenly point out every little mistake he observes—and there are quite a few. He might also become an unbearable know-it-all.

Can I Help Blues to Manage Their Stress?

They need privacy. They must be given time and space to think. They want to analyze the situation and understand the connections, and they need to be given time to do just that. If you give them space, they will come back—eventually. But if they fall too deeply into a funk, you may need to offer them more proactive help.

Conclusion: What can we learn from studying different people under stress? When under stress an individual's normal conduct and behavior are reinforced and exaggerated. A Red becomes even tougher and more aggressive towards those around him, a Yellow becomes more sulky and unstructured, a Green becomes even more passive and non-committal than usual, and a Blue can become completely closed and split hairs so thin that they're not even visible to the naked eye.

The most important thing is to avoid stressing people unnecessarily. Of course you knew that already, but it can be helpful to understand what actually causes stress for each profile. To push a Red is not as stressful as pushing a Green or a Blue. On the contrary, you have to push a Red for him to bounce back. If everything were to go smoothly, he would just get bored.

The situation, your profile, the time of day, the level of work, the group, the weather—lots of things determine stress in our lives. But if you pay attention, it will work out perfectly.

18

A Short Reflection Through History

People Have Always Been like This

The Background to Everything You've Read So Far

This chapter explains how I arrived at the research that forms the basis of the information in this book. If you're not interested in history, or references, or research, or things that take time from your otherwise full life, you can skip this chapter. For everybody else—a long time ago . . .

In all cultures, there has always been a need to categorize people. When the Stone Age period was over and we became more reflective as people, we discovered that all over the world people were different. What a surprise.

But how different are people really? And how have those differences been described? There are probably as many methods as there are cultures on earth. But I'll share some examples.

The Greeks

Hippocrates, who lived four centuries before Christ, is considered the father of medicine. Unlike many other physicians of that time, he wasn't superstitious. He believed that disease originated in nature and didn't come from the gods. For example, Hippocrates believed that epilepsy was caused by a blockage in the brain. Nowadays this is common knowledge, but back then it was revolutionary.

Humoral pathology, or the theory of the four humors or four bodily fluids, has to do with the four temperaments. According to Hippocrates, our temperament is the fundamental way we react. It's our behavior or our natural frame of mind. Our temperament controls our behavior.

Hippocrates believed that your health is good when the four humors—blood, yellow bile, black bile, and phlegm—are in balance. When we vomit, cough, or sweat, for example, the body is trying to rid itself of one or more of these substances.

The word *chloe* comes from Greek and means "yellow bile." Therefore, a choleric person is controlled by yellow bile or the liver. Fiery and temperamental, choleric people sometimes frighten those around them with their powerful ways. "Choleric" can be translated as "hot-blooded."

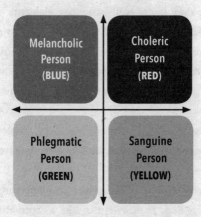

The Latin word *sanguis* means "blood." A sanguine person is controlled by the blood, by the heart. Creative and happy-go-lucky, he spreads positive vibes around him. Full of blood and therefore optimistic and cheerful, he has an airy manner. A synonym for a sanguine person is an optimist.

A phlegmatic person gets his influences from the brain. "Phlegm" means nothing more than mucus. Mucus is viscous, which symbolizes a phlegmatic person's temperament. A phlegmatic person is sluggish and slow in movement.

Finally, a melancholic person has an excess of black bile—the Greek *melaina chloe* simply means "black bile," found in the spleen—and is therefore often perceived as melancholic and gloomy. A common synonym for a melancholic person is a pessimist.

And there we have Hippocrates and his theories in a nutshell.

The Ancient People with an Eye for Color: The Aztecs

The Aztecs were a powerful people who lived in Central Mexico from the fourteenth century to the sixteenth century. They are known for their incredibly advanced civilization and impressive temples.

When they tried to divide people into different categories, they used something they knew well—the four elements: fire, air, earth, and water. To this day, the four elements are used to describe different frames of mind, but nobody really knows if the Aztecs were the first to actually come up with this idea. But we do know for a fact that they used this idea, because they left carvings illustrating this approach.

Fire people were exactly as it sounds: fiery, explosive, a bit hotheaded. They were warrior types who took to the sword to get their own way. Leaders.

Air people were different. They were also determined but considerably more easygoing. They swept in like a captivating wind, kicking up a little dust in the process.

Earth people worked for the village, for the collective. They had to

exemplify stability and security. They were there to create long-lasting things, to build for the future.

What about water people? Water was an element the Aztecs had respect for. Water can crush everything in its path, but you can also bottle it—if you know how to do it. Quiet and secure, water people observed everything that was happening.

As you can see, these divisions bear quite a resemblance to the theories propounded by Hippocrates—they're only different names for the same thing.

William Moulton Marston

William Moulton Marston created a systolic blood pressure test that was used in an attempt to detect fraud. The discovery resulted in the modern lie detector. But Marston was also the author of essays in popular psychology. In 1928 he published his work *Emotions of Normal People,* in which he investigated the differences in the behavior patterns of healthy people. Earlier, both Jung and Freud had published studies involving mentally unstable people, but Marston was a kind of pioneer who provided the foundations for what became known as the DISA model, the model that is the basis for this book. A few years after discovering Marston's work (in the 1950s), Walter Clarke developed the DISA concept based on Marston's observations. As you've seen, this is a model used to categorize the different types of human behavior. His work has been an endless source of valuable insights about behavior and human interactions, but it has not been without its critics. However, a great deal of work has been done since Marston's days, and over the years many other people have been involved in fine-tuning the DISA tool.

Marston found a way to demonstrate how people were different. He noted distinct differences between personalities, which formed the basis for the model used in this book. Nowadays we use the following divisions:

- Dominance produces activity in an antagonistic environment.
- Inspiration produces activity in a favorable environment.
- Submission produces passivity in a favorable environment.
- Compliance produces passivity in an antagonistic environment.

The four letters *D, I, S,* and *C* (Dominance, Inspiration, Submission, and Compliance) form the acronym of the DISC profile that is used throughout the world. Marston used the word "compliance"; however, in this book I render this as "analytic ability," as that better describes the type of individuals.

The *dominance* trait in any given individual relates to how he approaches problems and deals with challenges.

Inspiration refers to a person who likes to influence others. A person with this trait will always be able to convince others. In simple terms, you could say that dominance is about acting, and inspiration is about interacting.

The degree of *stability* is measured primarily by how receptive an individual is to change. A strong need for stability means a person is resistant to change, while someone who enjoys change will have a lower need for stability. This leads, of course, to a number of specific behavior patterns—like a nostalgic belief in the long-lost "good old days" for instance.

Finally, *analytic ability* shows how willing someone is to follow rules and regulations. Of course, this also produces certain characteristics that are interrelated. Here we find those who can't accept that things go wrong. Quality is important.

You've probably noticed that, regardless of whether it's a product of modern psychology or the ancient Aztecs in Latin America, these behavoral traits are all associated with the same color. The colors aren't critical; it's only a way to make it easier for those who aren't familiar with the system to make sense of the profiles. As a consultant, I've trained people in this topic for twenty years, and I've found that the colors facilitate learning.

Marston finished researching this topic sometime in the 1930s. Many others have used his research and developed a tool that, according to the most recent data, has been used by nearly 50 million people for the past thirty-five years. For example, the American Bill

Bonnstetter made invaluable achievements in creating definitive tools that help analyze the whole individual. In the United States, a company TTI Success Insights (ttisuccessinsights.com) offers a comprehensive analysis tool.

But it's always helpful to remember that though in theory there's no difference between the concept on the page and the practice, in the real world there's a big difference indeed.

I've described the four main traits that Marston pointed out, but remember that most of us are a combination of two colors.

19

Voices from Real Life

The book you are holding in your hands is a translation from Swedish of the fourth edition of *Surrounded by Idiots: How to Understand Those Who Cannot Be Understood*. When the Swedish edition was published, about fifteen thousand people in Sweden read it. I wrote this book because for many years in various context at training courses, lectures, et cetera, people always asked me, "Where can we read more about this system?" Up until now, the answer has always been nowhere. Then I wrote this book, and now you've read it.

As a writer, I always want to know what people think about what I have written. Because I also write fiction, I know how hearing the truth can be like an electric shock, but at the same time, I like to challenge myself. So, I interviewed four people with entirely different profiles, asking their views about the system itself but also about how they see their everyday lives—based on the color they have. As you read, pay attention to how they answer the questions (not just to what they say). You can learn just as much from how they respond as you can from the responses themselves.

Helena
CEO of a Private Company with Approximately Fifty Employees. Mostly Red, Without Any Green or Blue. A Small Dab of Yellow.

What do you think of this tool? DISA language?

I think it seems to be an effective way to avoid misunderstandings. I understood immediately what it was all about, so I think the book could have been shorter—half as long, maybe. I would have concentrated the text more. I don't like repetition. But sure, it's a useful tool. Last Christmas I gave a copy to all my coworkers as a gift and asked that they read it. And almost everybody did.

What is the most important takeaway for you from the book?

That I no longer have to beat around the bush. Now my staff know that I'm not an evil despot; I'm just Red. They understand that I'm not angry just determined. The most interesting thing was reading about Blue behavior. I'd never reflected on why they saw things so differently than I do. Now I understand that the process itself is important for them, which is why they take such a long time.

Anything else?

No. Well, Yellows. I've always wondered about them. All that babble. I have some acquaintances who are like that. They just sit down and blow a lot of hot air in your face without really saying anything much. My neighbor's like that. He plans all the time, but none of his plans actually take off. It doesn't bother me, but his wife must be insane by now. And at my company, the Yellows get too little done. But it's not a major problem, in my opinion. I just stand firm and demand that they deliver. I can live with their sour faces. I'm not there to be soft and cuddly.

What is your experience of Green behavior?

Sure. . . . Yes, well, what can I say? [Helena takes a long pause and looks out the window.] They're needed, too. Loyal and dutiful. But in all honesty . . . I'd never realized that they talk behind my back. But it's definitely true. They're phenomenal at spreading rumors. Even making the smallest change starts off a storm of gossip in the lunchroom. Speculations about one thing after the other. Usually completely incorrect and based on wrong information. It would be easier if they just came straight to me with their questions. I mean, how hard can it be to step into the manager's office and just ask? They know that I'll always answer honestly, so beating around the bush is frustrating. I don't know how many times I've said that we have to just be honest with each other at this firm. Is that so hard?

Why do you think they don't share what they're thinking with you?

They're afraid that I'll get angry, of course. I've never thought about it before. They think that I'm short-tempered, because, on occasion, I raise my voice or glare at someone, but that just means that I'm trying to highlight that what I've said is important. [Pause.] Personally, I couldn't care less if a conversation is a little tense; it's not the same thing as being angry. But it was news to me that some people actively avoid strong individuals. What I don't understand is how this happens between grown-ups.

You consider it immature behavior—not saying what you think?

Immature. Dishonest, actually. A lot like a child who refuses to admit that he took the chocolate chip cookie, even though he wasn't allowed to. I know that he did it, so what's the point denying it? That's something I really don't understand. Just admit your mistakes! Why is that so hard? Admit what you've done or not done, and then we can move on. But denying it or avoiding it . . . it drives me insane.

Okay. Let's consider the other colors. You said that you find Blues the easiest to deal with? Relatively easy with Yellows. But what about other Reds? How is it working with people that have the same profile you have?

Usually, no problem. We do what we have to do. I have a management team consisting of five people besides myself. I would say that three are Red. Or wait now. Two are Red and one Red/Yellow. One is Blue—the controller. And the last one is . . . hard to say. He's both visionary and at the same time focuses on the details. Can a person be Yellow/Blue?

Yes. A common combination. But no Green in the team then?
[Smiling.] No.

How does your Red behavior function, in general, do you think?

Well, before reading the book and discovering my personal profile I never thought that much about it. I hadn't really reflected on the way I approach things. But the more I read, the more I realized that I was the cause of some of the problems I've had at work. The thing about people hiding their real feelings was only one part of the story. It never occurred to me that some people were afraid or intimidated by the way I behave. There's been a lot of turbulence when I made decisions too quickly or when things weren't properly thought out. Of course, I know that I need to think through things before I decide on anything, but it just happens. I get an idea—and off we go! Implemented before lunch.

What are the consequences of these poorly thought-out decisions? Do you have any examples?

Tons. [Laughter.] Once I accepted a job without even asking about the salary. Turns out I had to work sixty hours a week without a penny in overtime. On one occasion, I hired a person who turned out to be totally useless. I hadn't asked for any references and I assumed that he knew what he was talking about. He knew nothing about the industry or the product. He was a complete scammer. Unfortunately, he cost us a lot before I finally managed to get rid of him. Lots of money wasted, though.

That doesn't sound ideal. How are things outside of work? How do you manage your personal relationships?

In those areas I think even less. But it's kind of funny. I showed the book to my husband and asked him to read it. He didn't, but I highlighted some areas that I insisted he read.

Red behavior?

Red behavior. And he did read some of it. He probably recognized his wife. He laughed a little, but now that I think about it, he didn't say anything in particular.

Did he make any comments about Green behavior?

No.

How do you work together? As a team?

How do we work together? [Loud laughter.] I tell him what needs to be done, and he does it. Before he's finished with it, I find something else for him to do and send him off to do it. Later on, I get annoyed because he hasn't finished. But he's never finished anything in his entire life. We often laugh about this—I create disorder but blame him. I'm sure he doesn't have an easy life.

I understand. What would you say your biggest challenges are, based on your Red behavior?

Some people take an eternity to make a simple decision, and it drives me crazy. I know I'm fast, but some people are just painfully slow. It doesn't make a difference if it's a friend or a coworker. For instance, we said that we were going to buy an armchair for our living room. Because I work so much, we agreed that my husband would [here Helena raises her eyebrows, and slowly a smile spreads across her face]. *I* agreed that he had to do all the research. Check online, furniture stores, secondhand shops, and so on. But nothing happened, of course! Two days later, when I asked him about it, he hadn't done anything at all! So, the following day during lunch, while I was in the bathroom, I found five different options and sent them to him. And when I got home five hours later, he still hadn't done anything! I exploded at him, and he locked himself in the basement.

Okay, a good example, thanks. How long have you been married?
Fourteen years. We met by chance. I usually say that what attracted me to him was that he could keep his mouth shut when needed, and he still does. But sometimes I wish that he would take a little more initiative and just do things. I've never actually asked him what he saw in me.

But how do you resolve your conflicts if he's Green and you're Red?
I don't think we actually have that many conflicts. On the whole, I'm the one who argues if anything happens, but, on the other hand, he can get very sulky.

What do you mean by sulky?
He can walk around for days just moping. Normally, I just ignore him; he usually recovers. But sometimes I get tired of all his sad faces and asking him what the problem is. I confront him, as it were.
[Pause.]

What happens then?

What happens then? Well . . . He says that there's no problem. That everything's great. But that's not true. He's really easy to read, so I always know if something is wrong. The problem is that he refuses to admit that he's grouchy. Which usually means that he's upset because of something I did. Or said. The problem is that I never remember anything. I have to start guessing—which is absolutely impossible. Often it's about some insignificant stray comment I made in passing, usually something I forgot the minute I said it. And if I don't guess correctly, then he gets even grumpier. It can go on for weeks. I don't understand how he copes with it.

But how do you move on? Can't you sort it out?

Well, we just tend to sweep it under the rug. I forget about the whole thing. But my husband stores the "conflict" in some private archive that only he knows about. That shelf must be completely full by now.

[Helena thinks for a moment. You know, I've always gotten in trouble for sharing my opinion, for walking my own path. I've never really fit in. Even as a child, I did stupid things and took risks. But now I'm glad that I took risks because it's taken me somewhere. But it definitely hasn't always been easy.

How has your risk-taking benefited you?

Sitting and thinking about things leads nowhere. It makes no difference how great your plans are if you don't get off your butt and carry them out. I didn't always know where I was going, but that never stopped me. I've had some tough spots, went bankrupt, lost my job, and things like that. Not that much fun, but those things brought me to where I am now. The way I see it, it's not how much you know or how clever you are, but what you actually do. And I have always been good at that. Doing things.

What advice would you give to people who meet you? What should they keep in mind?

[Pause.] Don't be intimidated by the fact that sometimes I'm a little too pushy. Don't back off just because I can raise my voice a bit. I'm not angry just because I push people. But also that they have to get the show on the road. My husband and I often talk about how different we are at delivering a message. While he gives the background for ten minutes and then comes to the point, I go straight to the point and tell people what's important. Maybe I throw in a little background info, but probably not. People should keep in mind that you can work without talking all the time. Put your energy into the task at hand instead of a bunch of other things. You can socialize on the weekend.

Håkan
Seller of Advertising Space on One of the Major Commercial TV Channels.
Mostly Yellow but with Some Splashes of Green. No Blue or Red.

What do you think of this tool? DISA language?

Really great! An incredibly useful tool that more people should know about. I recognized so much of myself in the book, too. It was brilliant. I showed the book to everyone I know, and we just had to laugh about how accurate it was. I've read most of the book, mostly about Yellows. I don't agree with everything, but most of it was spot-on.

What parts of Yellow behavior did you think were most accurate?

That we Yellows are very creative and resourceful. People are always telling me that. Also, I'm adept at solving complex problems, because I can see solutions in a different way than everyone else.

What do you mean by different?

Einstein once said that you can't solve a problem with the same mind-set as when you created it. Or something like that. I think that's exactly right. That's why I always approach any problem with new, fresh eyes. My customers always appreciate my creative thinking. And I'm really good at winning people over. I've always found it easy to charm people; it is a kind of natural talent actually. I know lots of people; I always have. And I'm great at public speaking. In school, I was president of the student council and often spoke to the entire school.

The entire school?

Yes, to all the students. Or not to all, not really. Okay, usually to my grade. All the freshmen. But there was always a great atmosphere, and people liked it. Since then, I just love talking in front of people. I'm often asked to be the spokesman in different contexts.

Can you give me some examples?

Oh yes. When there are projects at work, for example. I'm always the one to report back to our bosses. I give a great presentation at client meetings, too. If there are several of us from the firm, I do the talking.

What do the others think about that?

No problem. They like avoiding it. Lots of people have difficulty talking in front of people, as you probably know. Were you a psychologist? I know a girl who's a psychologist. She works at a prison; seems very interesting. She says most of the prisoners are pretty miserable, which isn't hard to believe. I wouldn't make it being locked away like that.

I'm not actually a psychologist. I'm a behavioral specialist.

There was one thing in the book that I didn't understand—areas for improvement.

What did you think that meant?

The book talked about how Yellows are quick to make decisions, and that's true. But I disagree with the idea that my decisions aren't well thought out. I'm very analytically inclined. I always do thorough research. I gather all the facts before I decide on anything. So in that regard the report book was off base.

I understand. Are there any other discrepancies?

That I use too many words when I criticize. That's completely wrong. I'm very concise and articulate, so I don't think that was accurate. Also the bit about following instincts and going with your gut—that's actually a good thing, not a weakness.

To go more on feeling than on facts?

Exactly. Humans are emotional beings. So we should use our feelings. Especially me. I'm very intuitive, so it's something I'm really good at. Not everyone has good instincts, so that's a real asset.

That may be true. Do you think people can develop their instincts over time?

No. It's something you're born with. You either have it, like me, or you don't.

Then it is too late to do anything about it?

No, it's not too late. That's was not what I meant.

But you said if people didn't have a gut feeling they couldn't develop that skill?

Okay, maybe I was exaggerating. But it's definitely important!

Do you ever need to keep emotions in check and use logic instead?

Oh yes, absolutely. It's very important to think logically and rationally. I always say that. You have to look at what works and go from there. I think that it's easier for someone like me, who has some experience. I have been a salesperson for many years, so I know what to take into account.

I'm sorry, but I am a little confused. Just now you told me that it was only gut feeling that was important. How do you reconcile those two things?

You're twisting my words. I never said that you shouldn't use logic. [At this point, Håkan crosses his hands over his chest and compresses his lips.] What I'm saying is that you should go on gut feeling. [Pause.] And facts.

Let's move on. What was the most practical thing you learned after reading the book?

That Blues are boring. Though I already knew that beforehand. I just didn't know that they were Blue. But those red-tape jackasses, well . . . I remember once I was working on this project. Nothing too complicated, and we'd already done the same thing before. A special way to sell a new product line. We had a couple of Blue guys on the team. They were smart, well informed, and everything, but they never got started on the job. They planned and wrote lists and made calculations and messed around with details. But they didn't actually do anything!

Maybe they weren't as good at using their gut feeling?

What do you mean?

So you find it hard to work with Blues?

They can't keep up with me, that's all.

Has what you learned in the book affected your personal life in any way?

No. I'm the same as I always. I've got lots of friends. The parties we organize at home are legendary. The neighbors talk about them for months afterwards.

So you invite the neighbors, too? That sounds very nice.

Oh, no way! They're boring as hell.

But what do the neighbors talk about then? If they didn't even come to the party?

[Pause.] Well, man, who knows? Ha-ha!

What advice would you give the people who meet you? What should they consider?

Who meet me?

Yes. How would you like those around you to react?

Let me tell you. Don't take life so seriously. I mean, we live only once. People should remember that. We should all let ourselves have fun at the same time. And don't caught up in little things all the time. Move on. Don't get hung up on things. I don't. Life's just a joyride.

Okay, that's what you believe. But what advice would you give to those who meet you? How would you like to be treated?

With a smile. You can get very far with a smile.

And when it comes to work? How would you like to be treated there?

Same thing I just said. With a smile. The rest will always work out.

[Pause.] Okay. There aren't any perfect people. We all have our faults and shortcomings, so what would you say your weaknesses are, do you think?

I don't usually think in that way. My focus has always been on positive things. I like to emphasize the good things in life. If everyone went around thinking about what doesn't work, then nothing would get done, right?

That's logical, but every behavior profile has weaknesses. They don't just go away because we avoid talking about them.

That's not what I mean. What I meant is that you shouldn't focus on negative things. It's better to emphasize the positive. God knows there's enough depressing stuff in the world already, right? Take, for instance, Green behavior. They worry about everything. They see danger absolutely everywhere. I mean, you can't go around being anxious all the time. It doesn't work like that. I have a neighbor who's afraid of everything. Especially new things, which are the things that I'm good at. Sometimes I think he's even scared of his own shadow. Or think about Blue behavior. Risk-phobic! Everything is a risk for them. Even if you know the result you'll get, they're still focused on the risks. That's totally incomprehensible to me.

You're absolutely right! Greens aren't inclined to change things, Blues get stuck analyzing risks. Do you see any weaknesses in Red behavior?

Cantankerous. That's what I think about Reds. Lots of them are actually quite nasty. Sure, they're result oriented and whatnot, but there's no need to be rude to get things done. Some of them can be so

short. You know, you send them a nice long text message, and the reply you get is just: "Okay." It takes five seconds to write a longer message, it doesn't cost anything, and it's so much more personable! I'm
always very careful about how I express myself.

**So you've analyzed the weaknesses in Reds, Greens, and Blues.
Do you think that there are any areas for development for Yellow
behavior?**

Yeaaah . . . it all depends on self-awareness. Without self-awareness,
things can get a little crazy. [Pause.]

Are you thinking of anything in particular?

The part about being a bad listener. That's important, 'cause if you're
not aware of it, then the conversation can go south. Though sometimes
you just can't sit around and listen. A lot of times I'm forced to take
command in meetings and run the show or else nothing will happen.
But I can keep things moving along, so it works out very well.

**Okay, so some Yellows can learn to listen better. What do things
look like for you? Do you think you have any weaknesses you could
be working on?**

[A very long pause sets in.]

Nothing that comes to mind.

Elisabeth
Employee at a Public Health-Care Organization
A Green with some Elements of Blue. She Has a Hint of Yellow but No Red at All.

What do you think of this tool? DISA language?

It was fun to read the book! I felt like I already knew a lot about
my behavior, but I think this has made it even clearer. Now I know

that Reds think I'm stubborn, and that I'm a bit cautious by nature. But I want everyone to be in agreement. Cooperation is important to me, and I think everyone should feel like that.

What did you take away from the book?

My son gave me the book as a birthday present. He's so kind, he always gives me something, even though I said I don't want any presents. He's unemployed and has some money troubles, but Filip is caring. It took me a while to get started reading the book. It was actually a little hard for me to get into it, mostly because I was interrupted all the time. But once I got going, I enjoyed it! There are such funny examples. I read the sections about my husband's colors aloud to him, and we laughed a lot.

What colors do you think he has?

Oh, he's Yellow. And Blue. At the same time, actually. Can someone be like that?

Yes. It's absolutely possible. What did you think was funny?

The parts about him being optimistic about time. He always believes that he'll get way more done than he actually does. And then we hit traffic the second we get in the car. Or he hops into the shower three minutes before guests start arriving. Things like that. But that optimism is part of the reason I fell for him thirty years ago. He's a good guy, my Tommy.

What will you take with you in the form of practical knowledge?

That I get on well with other Greens, which is good, because there are so many of us! I liked the part about how Greens take care of each other all the time. That's important. You've got to do that. But nowadays it feels as if everyone is becoming more and more selfish, but I don't think it will stay like that in the long run. I also read a lot about the Yellows, like my husband, and about Blues, like my sister. She is very straitlaced. Very rigid and a little bit uninterested.

Uninterested in what?

In the rest of the world, really. She never asks how things are going, and hardly calls you on your birthday.

Hardly calls? Does that mean she doesn't call you on your birthday?

Well, she does. But it feels like she's doing it out of obligation rather than out of genuine interest. And she can be really critical as well. Tommy redid our back deck a few years ago. Then Eivor came— she is my sister—and the first thing she did was start criticizing his work.

What did she say?

The first words out of her mouth were to point out that the deck railing was two degrees off from being level.

Was it?

Well, it was a tiny bit crooked. But why did she have to point that out? He'd been working on the deck for several weeks, and instead of complimenting his hard work, she just started criticizing everything.

So it wasn't just the railing that she criticized?

[Elisabeth shakes her head.]

What do you think about Reds?

Yes . . . they're okay, in their own way. [Pause.]

What do you mean?

They're very efficient. They get a lot done and they're quick. Sometimes I wish I had a little more of that ambition in me, but I don't. I'm just me.

But you think it might be helpful to be a little Red—sometimes?

Yes, sure. But you are who you are. And they can be a bit . . . tough.

How are they tough?

Well, a little bit insensitive in certain situations. Our department head is probably a Red. He'll say just about anything. And the surgeons are terrible to deal with. They boss people around however they want.

How does that affect you?

It's hard for me to deal with conflict. You can't avoid it completely, I know that, but it's difficult when everyone is butting heads all the time.

So everyone is at loggerheads all the time?

Not really everyone. And not all the time of course. But we definitely have communication problems. There's a bad atmosphere, and the management doesn't listen. A lot of us are suffering in that work environment. I was on sick leave last year.

Have you taken this up with your boss?

We tried to, five years ago. It didn't help much. It got better for a while, but then things just went back to normal.

Okay. So how are you feeling now?

It's all right. We have a great team of people at work, and that's important. We stick together. Many of us have been working there for a long time and we wouldn't want to leave.

What do you think about your own color? As a Green how do you get on with the other colors?

Well, the Reds are tricky of course. They don't like Greens, though there are a lot more of us. They complain about us; I've heard this personally. They say things; they call us names unnecessarily.

What do you mean by that? Can you give a specific example?

I don't have a specific example, but it's something you just know. You feel it when you're dissatisfied. It kind of hangs in the air.

You said that your boss was Red?

Not my immediate boss, but the head of the department. Emphatically Red.

And how do you know that?

Well, he is. It's clear as day. He walks quickly, talks quickly. Very demanding. Goal oriented. Difficult. He's made cuts.

If you implement cuts, you're tough?

Definitely.

So how are things going with the head of the department then?

I don't know. I've never spoken to him directly. But you just know.

You just know?

We've heard about other employees who got into hot water with him.

What happened then?

One of them has been harshly reprimanded for little things like arriving late. She was called into the office immediately. But not me. I'm always on time.

So someone didn't come on time for work and was criticized for that?

She got a telling-off.

What was said?

I wasn't there, of course, and didn't hear it, but she told me that it shouldn't have been handled like that.

Do you think it's okay to be late for work?

No, it's not okay.

But isn't it the head of the department's responsibility to correct behavior like that?

I guess so, but it depends on how you do it.

Did he scream and shout?

No, but he said that no one was allowed to be late, and if she came in late again, she would get a warning.

How many times had she come late?

Oh, she's never on time.

Okay. What would you like other people to know about you when they meet you in real life? How would you like to be treated?

Well, it would be great if people understood that some of us want to take it easy. And that I don't enjoy things changing all the time. I'd like to get a chance to get to know people a little bit before we just dive into work. Let's grab a coffee, chat for a while. It's nice to know people as people, and then we can get back to business.

Anything else?

Yes, we Greens aren't great at dealing with conflicts. We need to learn to handle that better.

Stefan
Economist Working at the Headquarters of a Very Large Company,
with Offices in Several European Countries.
Blue with Some Hints of Red. No Yellow or Green.

What do you think of this tool? DISA language?

It's quite an interesting concept. It seems like there's been a lot of research done on the topic, which I find exciting. I've seen a variation of this tool before, but that system categorized people by assigning different letter combinations. It would be interesting to compare the two models.

There are several different tools available. Most of them are grounded in the same basic research, but as time went on they developed differently. The tool I use is particularly accurate.

Do you mean with regard to reliability or validity?

Both. I'd also recommend Marston's book *Emotions of Normal People* if you're curious to learn more. What conclusions have you drawn after reading the book?

It was interesting to see how the author structured it. He wrote about Reds first, then about Yellows, Greens, and Blues. Each new topic was explained in reference to the four different colors. That was good because it means you don't get bored reading about any one specific color. And I noticed that there was always just about the same number of pages on each color, which is pretty impressive. I wonder how he managed it?

Regarding patterns of behavior, what have you learned so far?

That people are different. I knew that already, of course, but it was interesting to see exactly how we differ. And there were good examples in the book. For instance, I was particularly interested in Red behavior.

What are your thoughts on that?

Their tremendous drive to move forward. I have a colleague with exactly that kind of attitude and drive. Always moving forward, always first in line. His ability to make decisions quickly is very impressive. He ends up making a lot of mistakes, of course, but he corrects them quickly, so I don't think it's a huge problem.

Do you work well with Reds?

Pretty well, I think. Sure, they're often careless, as I said, but you can help them be more exacting. My role is usually to make sure we stick to the plan, and that's not something Reds are great at. But they're often quite good at improvising, which is a valuable skill. And they're brave.

It sounds as if you don't have any major problems with Red behavior?

No. It depends on what you mean by major, but I'd say I don't have any big problems with them. But, having said that, I think they have considerably more difficulty dealing with people like me.

What do you mean?

I want everything well structured. Zero mistakes. In this business, we work with finances and there's no margin for error. This industry demands a rather meticulous type of person. If I've understood the book correctly, Reds aren't interested in details, which is basically what my work amounts to. There would be enormous consequences if I were to be careless with decimal places. It just can't happen.

Okay. How about the other colors? How do you get along with Greens?

Fairly well. Both of us—at least according to the book—are introverts, which I think is a positive. Then you can devote yourself to work rather than just lolling around chatting. [Pause.]

But Greens like chatting.

That's true, they do. I don't, though. Unless it's work related. Then we can talk for a long time. What I don't like about Greens is that they have a tendency to make a pretense of working. They are often away from their desks, doing something else instead of working, and that slows everything down. It's a problem.

Do you find this is a common problem in your workplace?

Yes.

What have you done to tackle the problem?

Nothing.

Why not?

It's not my responsibility. It's a management issue.

Have you raised the issue with the management team?

No.

So some of your coworkers pretend to work, and this slows the whole team down. You've observed this but haven't done anything about it?

That's right.

But why not?

Like I said before, it's a management problem. I don't have any authority to act on the issue.

What would you do if you had the authority?

That's a hypothetical question.

Yes, but let's just say you did.

But that's not the actual situation. I'm not interested in management, so I don't know what I would do.

Just out of curiosity—if your boss asked you for advice on exactly this issue, an employee who doesn't do what they should, what advice would you give?

Purely hypothetically?

Yes.

I'd ask the boss to follow up with the problem employee more frequently. Give them feedback on what's not working, and demand that they change the problematic behavior.

Okay. Can we talk a little bit about Yellow behavior?

[At this point, Stefan crosses his hands on his chest and nods.]

How do you perceive people with distinctive Yellow behavior?

They're a bit annoying. I just wish that they'd take things much more seriously. Work, to start with. Of course, I realize that you also need to have fun at work, but not for the majority of the day. You can't fool around all the time during working hours. The worst thing is that they just wander around making a noise, bothering everyone. At times they can be very entertaining, but working is working and playing is playing. There's also the issue of their total inability to get the facts right. I think they're very incompetent when it comes to factual issues. They don't take anything seriously, and that leads to lots of mistakes. For instance, if a pure Yellow individual worked as a controller how would that work out? He wouldn't even know what to look for. But the really serious issue is that they say so many things that aren't true. For example, they might say that they double-checked certain details without ever actually doing it. Or insist that they're not careless despite the fact that everyone can see that they most definitely are. The whole thing is wildly frustrating.

Have you ever really gotten to know a Yellow?

How can you avoid it? They pour out their life story to whoever they like, with a total lack of discernment. They think that all of us are interested in their summer house, or their puppies, or their kid's new tooth, or their brother's new fishing boat. But all of that is completely and totally irrelevant.

Do you ever hang out with Yellows?

No. I tend to avoid them.

Why?

I wouldn't be able to stand all that talking. They'd talk me to death. I can't listen to them yammering on and on about everything and nothing. And you never know if what they're saying is actually true. That irritates me. They hyperbolize all the time; five minutes with a Yellow and I'm at my wit's end. My brother-in-law always talks about his new position at work. But he describes it differently every time. I've asked him what his title is, because I didn't understand what he actually does, but he always gets very vague. One time I asked how the company was growing and I got a long harangue about how they were just about to take out a world patent on something. But he wouldn't tell me how that was going to happen and what the details of the project were. It was hopeless.

Maybe he didn't know the answer?

Then he should have said so! "I don't know." I mean how hard can that be? Instead, he exploded with a hundred million things I wasn't interested in.

What advice would you give to others to help them interact better with you?

Good question. I'd advise them to please respect my desire to be professional and not devote valuable time to things that aren't work related. They should be well prepared when they come to me with questions. I need lots of background information to be able to give a proper answer.

What are your greatest weaknesses?

Let me think. Sometimes I get way too caught up in details. I know that. I don't think that it's an issue at work, but in my private life it can be a problem.

How so?

My wife is rather Red. She thinks that I'm slow at everything, and she's right. I tend to be suspicious of new ideas. Not that I can't change, but I often see problems where none actually exist. Sometimes I find it difficult to make decisions and I get anxious. We really need a new television at home, because the current one is on the fritz. But there are so many different models, and I haven't had the time to do proper research. My wife thinks we just need to take ten minutes and go buy a new one. But what if it isn't good? How do I know if it's the type we need? After all, it's a big investment. So we've just been making do with the old one.

Any last thoughts?

It's an interesting concept, as I said. I'm going to order the Marston book.

20

A Quick Little Quiz to See What You've Learned

Here's a chance for you to test your skills! This is a fun thing that you can use to test out your acquaintances. How much do you really know about how people work? I hope the answers you get will lead to interesting discussions, either around the water cooler or at the dinner table at home.

1. Which combination of profiles would naturally agree on a social level?

   Two Yellows

   Two Reds

   Yellow and Red

   Blue and Green

   All of the above

2. Which combination of profiles naturally work well together?

   Green with anyone else

   Two Yellows

   Two Reds

Blue and Red

All of the above

3. Which profile will always prefer to be the head of a project?

Red

Yellow

Green

Blue

4. Which profile would make the best surgeon?

Red

Yellow

Green

Blue

5. Which person would enjoy giving a speech the most?

Red

Yellow

Green

Blue

6. Which person would know exactly where he saved that email from his boss?

Red

Yellow

Green

Blue

7. Which person would want to do more tests or get more information before making a decision?

Red

Yellow

Green

Blue

8. Which person can you always rely on to arrive on time?
   Red
   Yellow
   Green
   Blue

9. Which person doesn't follow the rulebook to get a job done?
   Red
   Yellow
   Green
   Blue

10. Which person would be the most willing to try something new to get the job done?
    Red
    Yellow
    Green
    Blue

11. Which person will remember personal criticism the longest?
    Red
    Yellow
    Green
    Blue

12. Which person is the least organized but knows exactly where to go to get what he needs?
    Red
    Yellow
    Green
    Blue

13. Which profile always wants to make decisions?

    Red

    Yellow

    Green

    Blue

14. Which profile wears the latest fashions?

    Red

    Yellow

    Green

    Blue

15. Which profile would enjoy new challenges the most?

    Red

    Yellow

    Green

    Blue

16. Which profile would be the quickest to judge other people?

    Red

    Yellow

    Green

    Blue

17. Which combination of profiles would form the best team?

    Two Greens

    Two Reds

    Yellow and Red

    Blue and Green

    A mixture of all the colors

18. Which profile will probably talk the most?

Red

Yellow

Green

Blue

19. Which profile would assimilate new ideas the quickest?

Red

Yellow

Green

Blue

20. Which profile would delegate a task but then still do it himself?

Red

Yellow

Green

Blue

21. Which profile is the best listener?

Red

Yellow

Green

Blue

22. Which profile wouldn't miss the last step of the instructions?

Red

Yellow

Green

Blue

23. Which profile is most common in your social circle?

Red

Yellow

Green

Blue

The answers can be found on page 269.

More About Question 23

At work, you can't always choose the people you'll work with. They're just there, whether you would have chosen them or not. In the professional world, you have to play a good game with the cards that you have. But outside of work, when you can choose who you will spend your time with, what kind of people do you choose? Have you chosen people who are similar to yourself, or do you hang out with people who are your total opposite?

Of course, there are no right or wrong answers, but it's interesting to think about it. When we can choose, whom do we choose?

And how do we choose the partner we want to spend the rest of our lives with? Your mirror image, or your opposite? A fascinating question, right?

21

A Final Example from Everyday Life

Perhaps the Most Enlightening Team Project in the History of the World

Okay, my friend—it's time to summarize all of this. To do that, I'd like to tell you about a fascinating experience I had a few years ago.

I was leading a conference, and I got it into my head to do an experiment with a group of managers who were working at a telecom company. The participants were professional and clever, and all of them were successful in their respective fields. They had excellent qualifications and were destined for brilliant careers. I'd already made profiles for all of them—they had completed a self-assessment that showed which communication style they had.

I divided the managers into groups with similar behavior profiles. I imagined that it would be easy for them to get along. They'd certainly understand one another. There were twenty people in total. I called the groups Red, Yellow, Green, and Blue. I mean I had to call them *something*.

They had to solve a specially constructed problem that was connected to their field and required cooperation. They were given an hour to complete it. I explained the challenge and all the groups eagerly accepted the instructions and got to work.

After the groups had been working for a while, I went around and checked out what was going on in the various teams.

In the Red Group, the noise level was high. Three people were standing and loudly explaining why they were right. Two of them were in the middle of an argument, while the final person had decided to work alone. Completely unconcerned about the shouting match three feet away, he was writing so fast that his pen was starting to spark.

When I asked if everything was okay in there, everything suddenly stopped and all of them looked at me in surprise.

"Is everything okay?" I repeated anxiously.

"Peachy!" one of the belligerent guys said grimly. "We're almost done here."

I left them and continued on. The Yellow Group was also working frantically. You could almost taste the energy in the room. Things were happening! The discussions were lively, with everyone trying to convince the others of their own position. While the Reds were mad as hell with one another, there was nothing but smiles here. Three of the Yellows were jockeying for space at the whiteboard, and another told me an amusing anecdote that had nothing to do with the subject at hand (but it was actually hilarious). The fifth manager in the Yellow Group was doodling on a piece of paper and sending emails on his cell phone.

I left them to pay a visit to the Green Group. Inside the room, there was a strange calmness. Their voices were quiet, and they were all listening rather than speaking. The chief goal was stability and security. Five of the managers were sitting quietly, listening to one of their colleagues telling a sad story about his dog who had tragically died of old age that same winter. He was still missing his life companion.

The last manager had sketched out some suggestions about how they could solve the task I'd given them, but every suggestion ended with a question mark. She needed more input, and it looked like she would have to ask for it. She was in trouble.

I continued on. In the last group, the Blue Group, the room was almost absurdly quiet. After sitting with them for three minutes without anyone uttering so much as a single word, I was seriously concerned. A lot of thought was happening under the surface, but there was no real communication taking place.

A woman was reading silently through the task with her lips moving. I asked if they needed help to get started. I got a few hesitant nods in reply. They soon began a very thorough deliberation. They would absolutely get to the bottom of things. It was obvious that they were on the right track, but on an extremely detailed level. They discussed for a long time what their plan of action should be.

I remember glancing furtively at the clock. Half the allotted time had passed, but they hadn't produced anything concrete. Proposals had been put forward, but they'd been rejected by the others on a variety of technicalities. Every word was chosen carefully and the advantages and disadvantages weighed carefully. They were far more interested in doing things properly than in actually getting things done.

I left them to their fate and went back to the large conference room.

Before the allotted time was up, the Red Group arrived with triumphant grins. They congratulated one another for being the first back. They'd clearly won the test.

I had to go and fetch all the other groups. The Yellow Group was the slowest. I had to go back twice before they deigned to make an appearance. Two of them were talking on their phones, and the third guy only managed to recover after having some coffee and cake.

When all the groups had returned, I let them present their work.

The Red Group went triumphantly to the podium. They'd turned the task into a race. They were ready in thirty minutes, even though they had been given an hour. The rest of the time they'd spent phoning around to their coworkers, checking what they were doing with their time. It was a sound presentation, a well-organized structure, and properly thought out. But about thirty seconds into the report, it was clear that the Red Group had solved a completely different problem than what I'd given them. It wasn't at all what I had asked for.

When I asked if they had actually read the instructions, they all began arguing. One of the men stated confidently that they'd adapted the task to reality. They'd done a brilliant job. He expected applause, but when the standing ovation didn't materialize, the members of the group shrugged their shoulders and returned to their seats. A second after sitting down, the woman in the group began playing with her phone. A vital text message had to be sent immediately.

After that, it was the Yellow Group's turn. This group consisted of three women and two men. All of them smiled and stood at the front. Who should begin? A brief deliberation took place before one of the women charmed her way to the podium. She quickly plunged into her topic, presenting the exciting discussions they'd had for the past hour. She spoke for a while about the whole thing being an inspirational exercise; she described how she was going to use the insights she'd gained when she returned to her work. Her presentation was very entertaining, and everyone laughed. I was also amused by the woman's story, especially considering that it only had one purpose: to camouflage the fact that the group hadn't solved the task. However, the Yellow Group did manage to get some applause, mostly due to the high entertainment value of their presentation.

Now it was time for the Green Group. It took a while to get everyone up to the podium. While the Yellow Group had squabbled about who was going first, the Green Group was anxious. "Do all of us go up?" "Who should present the report? Should I?" "Shouldn't you do it?" At least half of the six participants looked as if they had a stomachache. Sure, this was the largest group but, nevertheless, they were all nervous.

No one took command. After a moment of low-key deliberations, one of the men began to speak. He faced the whiteboard most of the time. He talked softly, turning towards the members of his team for support. He was so subtle in his observations that the message was hopelessly lost. With growing desperation, he looked at his team for help.

When their presentation was over, not even the Green Group had solved the task, even though they had made more progress than the Yellow Group. I asked if everyone in the group was in agreement about the material that was presented.

The unfortunate spokesperson said that he thought that it was *probably true that most of them were relatively in agreement*. I asked the group, and they all nodded in unison. At least four of the participants in the group had grim faces, their arms crossed tightly around their bodies—body language that proclaimed they were far from agreeing with what had been said. One of the women looked resentfully at the spokesperson. But, by Jove, she was in agreement.

Finally, the Blue Group marched up in line and stood in alphabetical order, according to a prearranged agenda. Arne went through the instructions, revealing that there were several points that had made the task challenging. Among other things, he remarked on the sentence structure in the document that I had handed out—he spent most of the time explaining that it was better to say "advisor" rather than "adviser," although both forms are technically correct—and pointed out no fewer than two additional grammatical errors, on the very first page.

Then it was Berit's turn to go through the structure they had based their work on, after being interrupted twice by Arne, who believed that a few minor details needed to be clarified. When Kjell took over, they still weren't even close to providing a solution to the problem. Stefan didn't straighten out any issues, and when Yolanda finally announced they needed more time to finish the task properly, chaos erupted in the conference room.

The Red Group quickly branded the members of the Blue Group complete idiots, the Yellow Group felt it was the most boring thing they'd ever experienced, and the Green Group just suffered silently through the whole show.

Conclusions

The purpose of the whole exercise was to highlight that no group should be composed solely of individuals of the same type. Diversity is the only possible route. The best way to put a group of people together is by mixing different types of people. This is the only way to achieve decent dynamics in any group. This seems intuitive, but despite this, most of the organizations I have encountered fail on this fundamental requirement when they recruit people. Managers bring in new people who are just like themselves because they understand each other.

This book has been about explaining exactly why the groups in this example worked the way they did and giving you the tools to avoid similar problems in your own life. I hope that you found pleasure in reading it and joining in this exciting exploration of how people function, what makes them similar, and what makes them different. Because we are all different. If you keep your eyes open, you'll find out exactly how different.

The rest is up to you.

The Answers to the Questions
in Chapter 20

1. Two Yellows
2. Green with anyone
3. Red
4. Blue
5. Yellow
6. Blue
7. Blue
8. Blue
9. Red
10. Yellow
11. Green
12. Yellow
13. Red
14. Yellow
15. Red
16. Red
17. A mixture of all the colors
18. Yellow

19. Red
20. Red
21. Green
22. Blue
23. To this there is no given answer, as you might understand.

Further Reading

Blink: The Power of Thinking Without Thinking by Malcolm Gladwell. New York: Back Bay Books, 2007.

Conversation Transformation: Recognize and Overcome the 6 Most Destructive Communication Patterns by Ben Benjamin, Amy Yeager, and Anita Simon. New York: McGraw-Hill Education, 2012.

Emotional Intelligence: Why It Can Matter More Than IQ by Daniel Goleman. New York: Bantam, 2005.

Feel the Fear . . . and Do It Anyway by Susan Jeffers. Numerous editions.

Get Your Sh*t Together: How to Stop Worrying About What You Should Do So You Can Finish What You Need to Do and Start Doing What You Want to Do by Sarah Knight. New York: Little, Brown and Company, 2016.

How to Stop Worrying and Start Living by Dale Carnegie. New York: Gallery Books, 2004.

How to Win Friends and Influence People by Dale Carnegie. Numerous editions.

Influence: The Psychology of Persuasion by Robert Cialdini. New York: Harper Business, 2006.

Outliers: The Story of Success by Malcom Gladwell. New York: Back Bay Books, 2011.

Quiet: The Power of Introverts in a World That Can't Stop Talking by Susan Cain. New York: Broadway Books, 2013.

Social Intelligence: The New Science of Human Relationships by Daniel Goleman. New York: Bantam, 2007.

The 7 Habits of Highly Effective People: Powerful Lessons in Personal Change by Stephen R. Covey. Numerous editions.

The 10 Dumbest Mistakes Smart People Make and How to Avoid Them: Simple and Sure Techniques for Gaining Greater Control of Your Life by Arthur Freeman. New York: William Morrow, 1993.

The Power of Habit: Why We Do What We Do in Life and Business by Charles Duhigg. New York: Random House, 2014.

The Ten Types of Human: A New Understanding of Who We Are, and Who We Can Be by Dexter Dias. London: Random House UK, 2017.

Types of Men by Eduard Spranger. Scottsdale, AZ: Target Training International, 2013.

Index